Harbingers of Twentieth-Century Neo-classicism

Harbingers of Twentieth-Century Neo-classicism

Finn Egeland Hansen

Aarhus University Press

Harbingers of Twentieth-Century Neo-classicism
© Author and Aarhus University Press 2019
Cover: Sigrid Astrup Haraldsen
Layout and typesetting: Ryevad Grafisk
Publishing editor: Leif V.S. Balthzersen
Language editor: Gillian Fellows-Jensen
This book is typeset in Sabon LT Std and printed on 120g Munken Lynx
Printed by Narayana Press, Denmark

Printed in Denmark 2019

ISBN 978 87 7184 711 6

Aarhus University Press
Finlandsgade 29
DK-8200 Aarhus N
Denmark
www.unipress.dk

Published with the financial support of: VELUX FONDEN

International distributors:

Oxbow Books Ltd.
The Old Music Hall
106-108 Cowley Road
Oxford, OX4 1JE
United Kingdom
www.oxbowbooks.com

ISD
70 Enterprise Drive, Suite 2
Bristol, CT 06010
USA
www.isdistribution.com

PEER REVIEWED

/ In accordance with requirements of the Danish Ministry of Higher Education and Science, the certification means that a PhD level peer has made a written assessment justifying this book's scientific quality.

CONTENTS

1.	**Preliminaries**	**7**
1.1	Classicism versus romanticism	7
1.2	Implied structure of textbooks on 19th-century music history	8
1.3	The Thesis	8
1.3.1	Comments on Ferchault's article	13
1.4	Saint-Saëns' Aesthetical Preferences	14
2.	**Charles Gounod (1818-93)**	**19**
2.1	The Symphonies	19
2.2	Gounod's Masses	24
2.3	Other Vocal Works	44
3.	**Camille Saint-Saëns (1835-1921)**	**48**
3.1	The Symphonic Works	48
3.2	Piano Music	68
3.3	The Chamber Music	71
4.	**Niels W. Gade (1817-1890)**	**75**
4.1	String Quartets Nos. 1 and 2	75
4.2	Cantata *Zion*, op. 49	80
5.	**Neo-classicism**	**91**
6.	**Parenthesis on the Danish composer Paul von Klenau (1883-1946)**	**104**
7.	**Conclusion**	**105**
	List of quoted literature	106
	List of music editions	107

*Dedicated in friendship to
the late Charlotte Bergsagel
and my valued colleague
Professor emeritus John Bergsagel*

1. Preliminaries

1.1 Classicism versus romanticism

It is generally accepted that the terms classical and classicistic denote "stability, repose, clarity, balance, self-reliance, objectiveness, traditionalism," whereas romanticism expresses the sense of "unrest, exaggeration, experimentation, ostentation, diffusion, subjectivism, etc."[1] In the brief Danish *Musikalske Begreber*[2] under the article Romantik (Romanticism) the following words are inspired by the *Harvard Dictionary*:[3] "Classicism indicates the will to exercise moderation, balance, clarity and selfcontrol (the artistic creations of the Renaissance are from this point of view the result of such efforts), while romanticism implies unimpeded expression, the subjective and excentric at the expense of formal balance (consequently also much baroque art)." And in *The New Grove Dictionary of Music and Musicians*, the article 'Romantic:'[4] "A term generally used, in music, to designate the apparent domination of feeling over order, whether applied to a single gesture within a Classical or Baroque structure, to an entire work emphasizing these tendencies or to the period of European music between approximately 1790 and 1910 (hence sometimes known as the Age of Romanticism)."

---

1. Willi Apel: *The Harvard Dictionary of Music* (hereafter *Harvard Dictionary*): Article Classicism.
2. Søren Sørensen, John Christiansen, Bo Marschner, Finn Slumstrup: *Musikalske Begreber*.
3. Original Danish text: "klassik betegner viljen til mådehold, til balance, klarhed og selvkontrol (renæssancens kunstneriske frembringelser bliver under denne synsvinkel resultater af en sådan stræben), mens romantik indebærer det uhæmmet udtryksbetonede, det subjektive og excentriske på bekostning af formel balance (således også f.eks. meget af den barokke kunst)." All translations are mine, unless otherwise stated.
4. *The New Grove Dictionary of Music and Musicians*, edited by Stanley Sadie (hereafter *The New Grove*).

1.2 Implied structure of textbooks on 19th-century music history

Most textbooks on Music History – at least those with which I am acquainted – imply a tripartition of the principal musical currents of the 19th century.

The first is a romantic current representing a natural development and amplification of the means of musical expression of the classical era. The development largely takes place within the framework of established musical genres such as symphony, sonata, concerto and a variety of chamber music genres, among which the string quartet occupies a privileged position.

The foremost representatives of this current – often labelled **classical-romantic** – are Mendelssohn, Schumann and Brahms and among the composers flourishing towards the end of the century Bruckner is often mentioned.

The second is the so-called **new-German** current, the essence of which may be summarized as attempts to allocate or attribute extra-musical meaning to the musical works, be it of a concrete nature as in programme music proper or more or less vague feelings or moods. With Berlioz as the initiator the leading composers of this current are Wagner and Liszt with Richard Strauss as a latecomer of formidable dimensions.

The third main current is a **national-romantic** current, characterized by its inclusion of elements extracted from local folk-music – instrumental or vocal.

Every corner of Europe, former Czechoslovakia, Poland, Hungary, Russia, the Nordic countries, not to forget Great Britain, contribute to this musical current with a number of excellent composers.

This tripartition of the principal musical currents of the 19th century shall be my point of departure.

1.3 The Thesis

My thesis is that the classical-romantic main current in fact represents two sub-currents, the one focusing on the *romantic* aspects, the other focusing on the *classical* aspects of its musical style. For the romantic end of the musical spectrum I shall retain the term classical-romantic, for the classicistic end I shall apply the term retro-classicistic.

I know of no precedent for the application of the term retro-classicistic; but here and there consciousness of the existence of different poles or positions within the classical-romantic style is shown. So even if it is generally agreed to classify Mendelssohn, Schumann and Brahms as classical-romantic composers, scholars have for a long time hinted at the question: but what are each of these composers mostly: classicistic or romantic?

"Neither these various influences nor the composer's own comments about his music permit any definitive classification of Mendelssohn into the mode of thought of any particular period. Least of all is it tenable to call him a Romantic; on the contrary, his affiliations with the 18th century, especially the music of Mozart, make him if anything a neo-classicist."[5] "The romantic spirit leads even with him to an accentuation of the feeling of mood (experience of nature colours some of his most important works) but his music never becomes extemporaneous or unimpededly expressive and it retains nightly mystery and demonism, which greatly attracted that age, at a considerable distance."[6]

In *The New Grove* the following is said about Robert Schumann: "he did not cease to be a Romantic, but his Romantic conception of music first as a medium of self-expression was now modified by the older Classical view of musical composition as a craft to be practised."[7] "Schumann's straining of the romantic was intimately connected with the past, and his style must unite three historical components, which may be characterized as the following types, the character piece, the classical symphony and the baroque fugue."[8]

And about Brahms: "Concentration on essentials, absence of exuberant gestures and moderation in the choice of his medium define Brahms more as a renovator of tradition than as a reactionary symphonist."[9] "That this musical language, which in spite of the multitude of impulses fundamentally adheres to the contemporary stylistic tradition, has often been perceived as retrospec-

---

5. Article 'Felix Mendelssohn' by Karl-Heinz Köhler in *The New Grove*, section 8. The Work: Basic Concepts, Trends and Influences.
6. Article 'Felix Mendelssohn Bartholdy' in *Sohlmans Musiklexikon* (hereafter *Sohlmans Musiklexikon*): Original Swedish text: "Den romantiska tidsandan leder även hos honom till en betoning av stämningsmoment (naturupplevelser färgar några av hans viktigaste komp.), dock blir hans musik aldrig vare sig improvisatorisk eller hämningslös, och den håller sig också fjärran från det nattligt gåtfulla och demoniska, som i så hög grad attraherade hans samtida."
7. Article 'Robert Schumann' by Gerald Abraham in *The New Grove*, section 23. Orchestral and Chamber Music.
8. Article 'Robert Schumann' in *Die Musik in Geschichte und Gegenwart* (hereafter *MGG*): Original German text: "Schumanns Überdehnung des Romantischen hing auf das Innigste zusammen mit der Vergangenheit, und sein Stil mußte drei historische Komponenten in sich vereinigen, die sich in Typen bezeichnen lassen als das Charakterstück, die klass. Symphonie und die barocke Fuge."
9. Article 'Johannes Brahms' in *The New Grove*, end of section 10. Orchestral Music.

tive (even reactionary) depends not, however, alone on the many-sidedness of connections with older models and stylistic patterns, but to a great extent also on the music's way of expression."[10] "Later – in 1860 – Brahms signed a declaration against Listz and his circle, and after in 1869 he had been violently attacked by Wagner in the article *On Conducting*, both the personal and aesthetical conflict between Brahms and the new-German composers was a reality."[11] "Johannes Brahms was the great conservative of the Romantic era. He avoided such pianistic displays as Chopin's elegant ornamentation and Liszt's brilliance and rhetoric; his models, rather, were Beethoven and Schumann. Technically his piano style is characterized by full sonority, broken-chord figuration, frequent doubling of the melodic line in octaves, thirds, or sixths, multiple chord-like appoggiaturas, and considerable use of cross-rhythms."[12]

The European location best suited for studying this issue is France, which several times in the course of music history has been in the forefront of stylistic development.

The article about 19th-century France in the first edition of *MGG* (1949-86) is written by Guy Ferchault[13] and structured as follows:

"1. Music during the revolution and the Imperial Empires
2. Influences from abroad
3. The national factors
4. The great currents of the 19th century
    a. The romantic current
    b. The new-classical current
    c. Individualistic tendencies

---

10. Article 'Johannes Brahms' in *Sohlmans Musiklexikon*: Original Swedish text: "Att detta tonspråk, som trots impulsernas mångfald i sina grunddrag givetvis ansluter sig till samtidens stiltraditioner, så ofta har uppfattats som retrospektivt (eller t o m reaktionärt) beror emellertid inte enbart på denna mångsidiga anknytning till äldre förebilder och stilmönster utan i hög grad även på musikens uttryckskaraktär."
11. Article 'Johannes Brahms' in *Gads Musikleksikon* edited by Finn Gravesen and Martin Knakkergaard (hereafter *Gads Musikleksikon*): Original Danish text: "Senere – i 1860 – var Brahms medunderskriver på en erklæring mod Liszt og hans kreds, og efter at han i 1869 var blevet voldsomt angrebet af Wagner i artiklen *Über das Dirigieren*, var såvel den personlige som den æstetiske modsætning mellem Brahms og nytyskerne en realitet."
12. Donald Jay Grout and Claude V. Palisca, *A History of Western Music* (hereafter *Grout, Palisca*): p. 606.
13. In the new edition of *MGG* the article about France is replaced by a totally different one.

5. Development of musical genres
     a. The opera
     b. Symphonic music
     c. Chamber music
     d. The mélodie
     e. Church music
  6. Music institutions
  7. The interpreters
     a. Singers
     b. Instrumentalists
  8. Dissemination and reception of music
     a. Music publications
     b. Musicology and musical aesthetics"[14]

It is item 4 that especially calls for our attention. It opens: "Two main currents characterize the development of French music in the 19th century,

---

14. Article 'Frankreich, 19. Jahrhundert' in *MGG*: Original German text:
    "1. Die Musik zur Zeit der Revolution und des Kaiserreiches
    2. Die fremden Einflüsse
    3. Die nationalen Faktoren
    4. Die großen Strömungen des 19. Jh.
       a. Die romantische Strömung
       b. Die neuklass. Strömung
       c. Die individualistischen Tendenzen
    5. Die Entwicklung der Gattungen
       a. Die Oper
       b. Die symphonische Musik
       c. Die Kammermusik
       d. Die mélodie
       e. Die Kirchenmusik
    6. Die Musikinstitutionen
    7. Die Interpreten
       a. Die Sänger
       b. Die Instrumentisten
    8. Kenntnis und Verbreitung der Musik
       a. Die Musikpublikationen
       b. Musikwissenschaft und Musikaesthetik"

romanticism with Berlioz and César Franck as poles, and new-classicism with Saint-Saëns and Gounod as the most prominent composers."[15]

Item 4a first describes Berlioz and his influence on programme music. The section on Berlioz ends with the following sentence: "The spirit of absolute music remained alien to him."[16] This leads on to César Franck and his symphonies and chamber music. Berlioz and César Franck are seen as poles in French music, both romantic and consequently in opposition to that which the article labels *The new-classical current*.

4b in full[17]: "*The new-classical current*. Perhaps as a reaction against the unrestrainedness of romanticism there appeared a tendency, endeavouring to return to the classicistic principles, seeking balance of form and matter and clarity of style, and keeping a certain reservation by way of expression.

---

15. Article 'Frankreich, 19. Jahrhundert' in *MGG*: Original German text: "Zwei Hauptströmungen charakterisieren die Entwicklung der frz. Musik im 19. Jh., die Romantik deren äußerste Pole Berlioz und César Franck darstellen, und die Neuklassik, deren markanteste Vertreter Saint-Saëns und Gounod sind."
16. Article 'Frankreich, 19. Jahrhundert' in *MGG*: Original German text: "Der Geist der absoluten Musik blieb ihm unbekannt."
17. Article 'Frankreich, 19. Jahrhundert' in *MGG*: Original German text: "*Die neuklass. Strömung*. Vielleicht als Reaktion gegen die Hemmungslosigkeit der Romantik zeichnete sich eine Tendenz ab, die sich um Rückkehr zu den klass. Prinzipien bemühte, indem sie Gleichgewicht von Form und Gehalt und Klarheit der Schreibweise suchte und sich eine gewisse Reserve im Ausdruck auferlegte. Gounod und Saint-Saëns sind, von einigen Kleinigkeiten abgesehen, als Vorkämpfer dieser Richtung zu betrachten, durch die sie die frz. Musik neuen Zielen zuführten. – Grandioses, Fantastisches und Spukhaftes sind bei Gounod nicht vorhanden. Aber die Geschmeidigkeit seiner Melodik, die etwas schmachtende Anmut seiner Arien und der Charme und die Ungezwungenheit, die von ihnen ausgehen, geben seiner Musik einen vertraulichen und innigen Ton und gleichzeitig eine Vornehmheit, für die man schon den Sinn verloren zu haben schien. Sein Schaffen ist nicht frei von Gefallsucht, aber er geht dabei nicht so weit, sich zu erniedrigen. Gounod brachte in das Reich der *mélodie* und des lyrischen Theaters durch seine Art ein neues Element, das der Musik Gewicht und Gehalt gab, worum man sich in diesen Gattungen seit fast einem halben Jh. nicht mehr gekümmert hatte.
– Saint-Saëns war vielleicht weniger inspiriert, bewies aber zweifellos größere theoretische Kenntnis und verfügte über ein bemerkenswertes Können. Er brachte die formalen und technischen Eigenschaften der Musik wieder zu Ehren. Sein Schaffen ist von einer gewissen Strenge, in der sich die Forderungen seines schöpferischen Denkens und der Wille zur Vollkommenheit wiederspiegeln, den er an die Kunstübung herantrug. Aber diese Gediegenheit war nach der Erschlaffung der Revolutionsperiode und der romantischen Ära sehr heilsam. Durch seine Strenge trug Saint-Saëns dazu bei, den frz. Musikern Geschmack an vollkommener Form, an schöner Technik und edler Architektonik wiederzugeben."

Apart from some minor composers Gounod and Saint-Saëns must be considered champions of this current through which they provided French music with new goals.

The grandiose, fantastic and spooky are not present in Gounod's music. But the suppleness of his melodies, the somewhat languishing pleasantness of his arias, and the charm and unaffectedness, which emanate from him, give his music a familiar tone and at the same time an intimate dignity, for which one already seems to have lost understanding. His creations are not devoid of coquettishness, but in this he never goes so far as to abase himself. Gounod gave through his art the realm of *mélodie* and the lyrical theatre a new element that gave weight and substance to music, to which one for almost half a century had payed no attention.

Perhaps Saint-Saëns was less inspired, but undoubtedly he possessed greater theoretical knowledge and was remarkably able. He brought the formal and technical elements of music back to an honourable standing. The creativeness which he brought to Art, is of a certain strictness, in which the demands of his creative thinking and his aim for perfection are reflected. But this purity was very healthy after the slackening of the revolutionary period and the romantic era. Through his strictness Saint-Saëns contributed to restoring to French musicians a taste for perfect form, beautiful technic and noble architecture."

1.3.1 Comments on Ferchault's article

The word *new-classical* in the heading of section 4b is inconvenient when used in connection with 19th-century music. *New* is translated *verbatim* the same as *neo*. And it is evidently not a musical current identical with the *neo-classicistic* current of the 20th century involving such composers as Igor Stravinsky, Paul Hindemith and the French group *Les Six*. I shall therefore propose that we replace the word *new-classicistic* in Ferchault's article with *classical-romantic*. As we shall see, we are talking about a musical way of expression in line with that of notably Mendelssohn but also other classical-romantic composers.

Also the word 'perhaps' at the beginning of section 4b leaps to the eye, but I think that Ferchault is too timid. Unrestrained (mis)use of musical resources (triple woodwinds, lots of brass, multiple harps, lots of percussion and correspondingly large groups of strings), unrestrained demands on the patience of the audience (works lasting hours), unrestrained musical expression (a harmonic language which not only threatens to, but eventually leads to the collapse of the harmonic system). This is what Ferchault questions with the word 'perhaps'.

1.4 Saint-Saëns' Aesthetical Preferences

Saint-Saëns (1835-1921) has given written utterance to his aesthetical preferences – and one may safely add – in a rather outspoken manner. Below are eight quotations from his *Outspoken Essays on Music*. They call for close reading and discussion; but in the present connection such an endeavour is unnecessary and may be perceived as a stopgap. Here they are:

1) First from the preface: " 'Primary' music, that which appeared simultaneously with the human race itself, consists of two elements: melody and rhythm. It held sway throughout Europe up to the time of the Middle Ages and still reigns throughout both the Near and the Far East. […]

'Secondary' music began its first feeble stammerings in Europe during the Middle Ages. […]

The early attempts of 'secondary'…. our own… music to express itself were very strange; there was much searching and groping of the way; the ear was often diverted from the right track to an extent that cannot easily be imagined. It was only by degrees that experience painfully worked out laws which, after being strictly observed for some time, have progressively widened out and extended their scope until the domain of music now covers an immense field of activity. In these modern times of ours, however, this expansion is no longer sufficient; these very laws are being repudiated and looked upon as never having been in force at all, as *non avenues*…"[18]

2) "By reason of his talent and erudition, by virtue of his position as the founder of a school, M. Vincent D'Indy has acquired great authority. Everything he writes must of necessity possess considerable influence.

Under the sway of such considerations, it has occurred to me that it might be useful to point out – even though it be to my detriment – certain of his ideas in the 'Course of Musical Composition' which do not agree with my own. Not that I claim to be a more or less infallible oracle; it does not fol-

---

18. Camille Saint-Saëns: *Outspoken Essays on Music*, Authorised Translation by Fred Rothwell (hereafter *Outspoken Essays*): pp. IXff.

low, because M. D'Indy's ideas are not always mine, that they are therefore erroneous [.] I will state my arguments: the reader shall judge for himself."[19]

3) "M. D'Indy, like Tolstoi and M. Barrès and many other thinkers, seems to see nothing in art but expression and passion. I cannot share this opinion. To me art is form above all else.

It is perfectly clear that art in general, especially music, lends itself wonderfully well to expression, and that is all the amateur expects. It is quite different with the artist, however. The artist who does not feel thoroughly satisfied with elegant lines, harmonious colours, or a fine series of chords, does not understand art.

When beautiful forms accompany powerful expression, we are filled with admiration, and rightly so. In such a case, what is it that happens? Our cravings after art and emotion are alike satisfied. All the same, we cannot therefore say that we have reached the summit of art, for art is capable of existing apart from the slightest trace of emotion or of passion."[20]

4) "In the introduction of his book, M. D'Indy says the most excellent things about artistic consciousness, the necessity of acquiring talent as the result of hard work and of not relying solely on one's natural endowments. Horace had said the same thing long ago; still, it cannot be repeated too often at a time like the present, when so many artists reject all rules and restrictions, declare that they mean 'to be laws unto themselves,' and reply to the most justifiable criticisms by the one peremptory argument that they 'will do as they please.' Assuredly, art is the home of freedom, but freedom is not anarchy, and it is anarchy that is now fashionable both in literature and in the arts. Why do poets not see that, in throwing down the barriers, they merely give free access to mediocrities, and that their vaunted progress is but a reversion to primitive barbarism?"[21]

5) "Fétis had foreseen the coming of the 'omnitonic' system. 'Beyond that,' he said, 'I see nothing further.' He could not predict the birth of cacophony, of pure *charivary*.

---

19. *Outspoken Essays*: p. 1.
20. *Outspoken Essays*: pp. 4f.
21. *Outspoken Essays*: pp. 6f.

Berlioz speaks somewhere of atrocious modulations which introduce a new key in one section of the orchestra while another section is playing in the old one. At the present time as many as three different tonalities can be heard simultaneously.

Everything is relative, we are told. That is true, though only within certain limits which cannot be overstepped. After a severe frost, a temperature of twelve degrees above zero seems stiflingly hot; on returning from the tropics, you shiver with cold at eighteen degrees above zero. There comes a limit, however, beyond which both cold and heat disorganise the tissues and render life impossible.

The dissonance of yesterday, we are also told, will be the consonance of tomorrow; one can grow accustomed to anything. Still, there are such things in life as bad habits, and those who get accustomed to crime, come to an evil end…"[22]

6) "The more civilization advances, the more the artistic sense seems to decline: a grave symptom. We have already said that art came into existence on the day when man, instead of being solely preoccupied with the utility of an object, began to concern himself with its form."[23]

7) "What sets me at ease in discussing the ideas of M. D'Indy is the fact that, as he himself confesses, these ideas are very frequently not his own at all, but rather those of Hugo Riemann, a German."[24]

8) "*Vocalises* are absent from the works of Richard Wagner, though he did employ the trill, or shake; and while the trills of Brünnehilde are very effective in the 'Valkyrie,' those in the duet with Siegfried, on her awakening, seem very strange to any in the audience who have not been sufficiently hypnotised by Wagnerian infatuation."[25]

A strong dislike of Wagner, faith in law and order in music, and much concern about the lawlessness implied by the romantic way of musical expression appears immediately from the eight quotations. Thus we may safely remove

---

22. *Outspoken Essays*: pp. 7f.
23. *Outspoken Essays*: p. 8.
24. *Outspoken Essays*: p. 9.
25. *Outspoken Essays*: p. 22.

the word 'perhaps' from the beginning of section 4b of Guy Ferchault's article and exemplify unrestrainedness, as I have done above.

Exactly what or who Saint-Saëns includes under the heading 'romanticism', which he argues against, is not immediately clear. The question is whether or not he includes classical-romantic music. Do Mendelssohn, Schumann and Brahms belong to the good company or to the lawless romantics? Saint-Saëns' view of the three great classical-romantic composers may be elucidated by his verbal accounts or through analyses of his musical works, supposing that he himself – at least to a degree – lives up to his own aesthetical preferences.

It is surprisingly little Saint-Saëns writes about Mendelssohn, Schumann and Brahms. What there is, is found in *Outspoken Essays on Music* and *Musical Memories*.[26]

"Robert Schumann, whose reason was not very clear – it is well-known that he died insane – took into consideration only his own will when he neglected the requirements of nature; along these lines he committed the greatest of errors.

One of his most characteristic aberrations is in the *Scherzo* of his famous Quintet [...]"[27] Here follows a critical analysis of Schumann's placing of bar-lines in his piano quintet, but nothing that may be taken in support of his general view of the classical-romantic music.

"Both Mendelssohn and Schumann tried the theatre. The failure of Schumann's 'Geneviève' – interesting as it was from a musical point of view, though anything but adapted for the theatre."[28] Not much to go on here either.

Page 116 in *Outspoken Essays*: "It may be divined that I am alluding to those, well known to be a numerous band, who flock to the banner of the mighty Richard, and beneath its shade engage in a fight that has long been inconclusive.

They are not content that their god should triumph; there must even be victims sacrificed on his alters.

Mendelssohn first of all. Certainly there is lack of uniformity in his work. But what of 'Elijah', the 'Midsummer Night's Dream', the sonatas for the organ, the preludes and fugues for the piano-forte, the Scottish Symphony, the Reformation Symphony?... Try to accomplish a like task!

---

26. Camille Saint-Saëns: *Musical Memories*, Translated by Edwin Gile Rich.
27. *Outspoken Essays*: pp. 10f.
28. *Outspoken Essays*: p. 25.

They would have us believe that when he first appeared he was accepted without a struggle, his 'mediocrity' having at the outset placed him on a level with the masses.

Do not believe anything of the kind.

I was present at the very first performance of the 'Midsummer Night's Dream' and of the Symphonies, given before a Parisian public, and I still remember that I broke more than one lance in his defence. At the first performances of the 'Midsummer Night's Dream' I saw old *habitués* of the Conservatoire holding their heads in their hands as they asked in tones of anguish why the Société des Concerts inflicted such horrors on its subscribers... Only by degrees did this public discover the Berceuse, then the Scherzo, then the Marche, then the Agitato, and finally the Overture. It was a tedious process!

Another victim: Meyerbeer. It was mainly against his 'Huguenots' that an outcry was raised, by reason of its popular and long unchallenged success. Robert Schumann lent powerful aid in this direction through an article he wrote which declared that the 'Huguenots' was not 'music.'

Unfortunately, when Schumann applied his marvellous talent to opera, he created 'Geneviève.' Now, 'Geneviève' is assuredly charming music, though of a kind ill adapted to the theatre. Henceforth, so far as the 'Huguenots' is concerned, Schumann's judgement is lacking in authority. On the other hand, we have the opinion of Berlioz – who is known to be anything but indulgent in criticism – and he in his famous 'Traité d'Instrumentation' quotes fragments of the great duo, 'cette scène immortelle.' This, in my opinion, is praise of no negligible kind."[29]

That Saint-Saëns does not include Mendelssohn among the 'bad guys' is clear enough. His opinion of Schumann is more ambiguous. Schumann is criticized on several accounts but nothing which is specifically directed at his general aesthetical preferences.

In *Outspoken Essays* there is not a word about Brahms.

We should now be prepared to start on our work proper, the analyses connected with the tracking down of retro-classicistic passages, movements, works in my endeavours to render plausible the thesis of this book. I shall concentrate on three composers, Charles Gounod (1818-1893), Camille Saint-Saëns (1835-1921) and Danish Niels Wilhelm Gade (1817-1890).

---

29. *Outspoken Essays*: pp. 116ff.

2. Charles Gounod (1818-93)

Even before Charles Gounod entered the Paris Conservatoire in 1836 he had received a thorough private musical education from Anton Reicha among others. At the conservatory the extremely talented Gounod was further educated by eminent teachers in counterpoint, composition and piano. He won the Grand Priz de Rome 1839 and subsequently travelled to Rome where he cultivated his profound interest in the music of Palestrina.

Owing to the outbreak of the Franco-Prussian War (1870-71) Gounod fled to England on September 13th 1870, and stayed there until 1874, when finally he returned to France.

2.1 The Symphonies

Petite symphonie pour instrument a vent

Gounod's *Petite Symphonie* for flute, 2 oboes, 2 clarinets 2 French horns and 2 bassoons was composed in 1885 and it is evidently a retro-classicistic composition.[30] Its immediate sonic appearance is that of an elegantly scored Viennese classical cassation, serenade or divertimento. Mozart, Franz Danzi and Anton Reicha are composers that come to mind.

The opening movement is cast in sonata form with a slow introduction followed by an Exposition section in agreement with the classical norms of this form. The first theme is in B flat major

---

30. Charles Gounod: *Petite Symphonie* for flute, 2 oboes, 2 clarinets 2 French horns and 2 bassoons.

and is repeated an octave higher (bars 24-28).

After a bridge passage the second theme appears in F major:

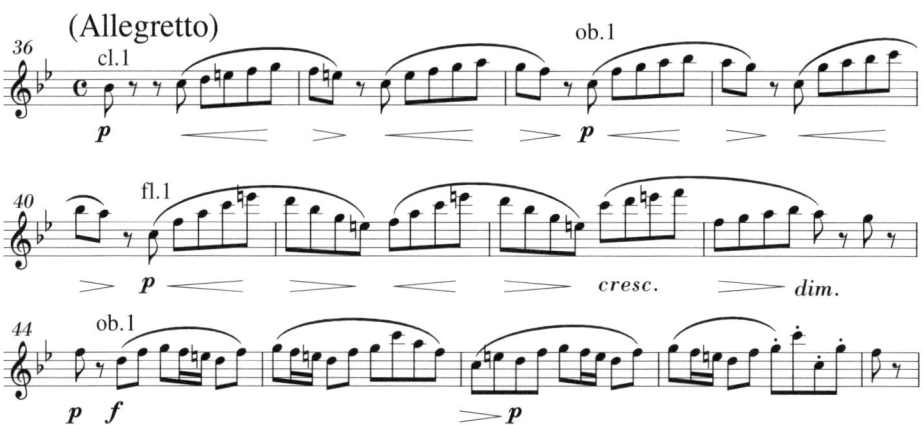

These F major passages may be analysed in more than one way. My suggestion is that we regard bars 36 to 40 beat 1 as part of the bridge-passage, bars 40 beat 2 to 44 beat 1 as the second theme and bars 44 beat 2 to 48 as a closing theme or motive. The Exposition is repeated.

The Development section (bars 50 to 96 beat 2) applies material from both themes. The shortened Recapitulation sets in bar 96 beat 3. It turns to E flat major (bar 100) but returns to B flat major during the presentation of the second theme (bars 106 to 110). Bars 112 to 122 are the Coda.

The second movement, *Andante cantabile*, opens with a seven bar introduction followed by a very long melodic line in the flute (bars 8 to 29). The key is E flat major. Then 34 bars of Development-like material (bars 30 to 63) are presented. Bars 64 to 81 are a slightly shortened and varied repetition of the long flute melody. The movement ends in E flat major with 8 bars of cadential motives.

The third movement is a Scherzo, *Allegro moderato*, 6/8 in B flat major.
    The Scherzo section consists of a 12 bars opening tuning in on B flat major followed by three repeated sections of 8, 20 and 28 bars respectively. The key is B flat major with modulation to closely related keys. The themes/motives are robust and clear-cut.
    The Trio section – although not labelled as such – is in E flat major and consists of 20 bars plus a repeated section likewise of 20 bars. The melodic line and the pedal points which lie under most of the trio together with the dry woodwind sound of the ensemble makes the Trio sound a little like a bagpipe.

The Finale is a sort of sonata form. The main theme is distinctive by an ascending leap of a fifth. The first 20 bars is an introduction ending on a dominant seventh chord to B flat major, with a fermata on the ensuing rest.
    Now follows a repeated section constituting the Exposition. The fifth is extended with a melodic line ending with a cadence in F major (bar 36). This is repeated in a different scoring and this time it ends with a B flat major cadence (bar 52). A bridge-passage motif leads in bar 89 to a C major cadence, and in bar 90 a variation of the main theme (main theme$_{var}$) is introduced, which brings the main theme group to a close in C major bar 97.
    The second theme in F major is presented in bar 98. It only reigns for 8 bars. Bar 106 a motif reminiscent of the bridge-passage motif leads to the main theme fifth in bar 110. Upbeat to bar 118 brings the bridge-passage motif, and bar 126 the Exposition closes with an F major cadence. The Exposition section is repeated.
    The Development section opens with an ascending leap of a major sixth, g flat – e flat, which may be perceived as a variation of the main theme and at the same time the greatest musical surprise in the whole symphony. The bridge-passage motif enters in bar 147 in D flat major. It reigns until bar 182, where it ends with an F major cadence. With bar 183 comes the main theme$_{var.}$ The main theme fifth reappears bar 191. Its cadence in B flat major

in bar 198 marks the beginning of a Coda, which in addition to a final presentation of the main theme fifth bar 207 brings a number of elegantly scored cadences in B flat major.

This finale may be described as a sonata form almost without its Recapitulation section which is represented only by the main theme$_{var}$ in bar 183 and the main theme fifth in bar 191.

Symphony No. 1 in D major[31]

Gounod wrote his first symphony in 1855. It has four movements.

The first movement, *Allegro molto*, is a sonata form with themes and motives which Gounod combines ingeniously and – particularly in the Coda – in a surprising way. However, surprise is provided by inventiveness, not romantic lawlessness.

The Exposition presents three themes, the main theme, the second theme and an epilogue theme in D, A and A major respectively. The Exposition is repeated. The Development section presents a new theme. The Recapitulation displays the three themes of the Exposition, here in D major all three of them as prescribed by the norms of the sonata form. The Coda is longer than one would expect and tends towards being a second Development section but the general impression of its style is classicistic and on the harmonic level it hardly goes beyond what one may encounter with the Viennese classical composers.

The second movement, *Allegretto moderato*, is based on two thematic ideas. The first, T1 in d minor modulating to F minor in bar 8, is presented by the strings *con sordino*:

It reigns until bar 48, where its conclusion is marked with a fermata. After eight bars of transition the second thematic idea, T2 in B flat major (likewise modulating to F major), is presented:

---

31. Charles Gounod: *Symphony No. 1 in D major*.

It takes the lead until bar 88 where a fugue with a subject derived from T1 is initiated:

The fugue ends bar 117, and after a bridge-passage T1 returns in the bass in bar 125 from where it controls the scene until the end of the movement (bar 175, d minor).

With a little stretch of the imagination this movement may be categorized as a sonata form with the fugue as the Development section and a Recapitulation without the second theme.

The Scherzo is cast in the normal form: two repeated sections in the Scherzo section and the same in the Trio. Its tempo, *Non troppo presto*, and time signature (3/4) is rather that of a Minuet, however. It sounds very much like Haydn, especially the pedal points in the Trio. The third relation between the concluding C major chord of the first section of the Scherzo and the A flat major chord which opens the second section, on the other hand, is typical of Charles Gounod's harmony.

The Finale is absolutely faithful to the norms of the sonata form. The 20 bar slow introduction, *Adagio*, is in D major, time signature c. The Exposition, *Allegro vivace*, presents a main theme in D major bar 25 in ¢. Bar 94 brings the second theme in A major. The Exposition is repeated.

The Development section introduces a new, lyrical theme, returns to the second theme in bars 208 (F major) and 214 (G major) and the Development ends in the same way as the Exposition and leads to the Recapitulation in bar 252.

The Recapitulation presents the main theme in D major (bar 252) and the second theme, likewise in D major, bar 313.

Bars 363-391 are the Coda.

Despite the formal anormalities in the first movement, I regard Gounod's *Symphony No. 1* as a retro-classicistic composition, its model being Haydn rather than Mozart – and only a little bit of Beethoven.

Symphony No. 2 in E flat major[32]

The second symphony (1856) is very much like the first, only somewhat larger. About 30 procent longer, the orchestra slightly larger. But the musical style is rather similar although definitely more inspired by the early Beethoven than the first symphony. So I do not hesitate to label Gounod's second symphony as a retro-classicistic work.

2.2 Gounod's Masses

Messe solennelle de Sainte Cécile[33]

This Mass, composed in 1855, is a classical-romantic concert mass with no trace of retro-elements, be it in the outer form or the inner style. Unusual with regard to its outer form is, however, the inclusion of an 'alien' text element, a text trope. After the first *Agnus Dei*, presented in four-part harmony, a tenor soloist sings: *Domine, non sum dignus, ut intres sub tectum meum sed tantum dic verbo, et sanabitur anima mea.* This text returns after the second *Agnus Dei*, this time sung by a soprano soloist to a slightly altered melody. In my opinion, however, it would be over-interpretation to understand this as a retrospective element. It should rather be interpreted as a typical romantic inclination to feel free of rules and formulas.

A close reading of this work is unnessessary, as its stylistic classification as classical-romantic is evident. However, I shall bring a single music example among an infinity of possibilities, namely some bars from the Kyrie:

---

32. Charles Gounod: *Symphony No. 2 in E flat major.*
33. Charles Gounod: *Messe solennelle de Sainte Cécile.*

Quatrième Messe Solennelle[34]

Gounod's own designation of his *Quatrième Messe Solennelle* (1888) is a *Messe Chorale sur l'intonation de la Liturgie Catholique*. This mass, however, is not built as any of the typical mass-forms of the *Ars Nova* period and the Renaissance, where the most common types of mass are the *cantus firmus* mass and the paraphrase mass. The *cantus firmus* mass is composed over a *cantus prius factus* forming the fundament of all five movements, even if it may be absent in shorter and longer passages of all movements. To begin with the *cantus firmus* was placed in the tenor in longer note values than the other parts; but gradually over time it is treated more freely. The *cantus firmus* is always an 'alien' melody, i.e. a melody taken from other parts of the Gregorian repertoire than the Mass Ordinary or it could be a secular melody. *Cantus firmus* masses built on the Maria-antiphon *Ave Regina Coelorum* is an example of the first and masses built on secular melodies such as the popular *L'homme Armé* an example of the second.

In paraphrase masses the original Gregorian melody from the Mass Ordinary is used, normally placed in the upper part in an elaborated form.

Gounod uses the identical intonations of three of *Graduale Romanum*'s six *Credo* melodies in a slightly altered form as the fundament of his *Quatrième Messe Solennelle*:

I have counted 50 appearances of this 'motto' in a composition with a playing time of about half an hour. This means that not one minute elapses without the motto being heard, and it is hardly too much to say that this *Credo* intonation dominates the work as much as does the *cantus firmus* of a cantus firmus mass proper.

Gounod varies his use of the motto, its rhythm, however, being unchanged, which contributes to its aural recognizability.

---

34. Charles Gounod: *Quatrième Messe Solenelle*. Throughout this work the time signature ₵ is rendered as C. The error is tacitly emended in the music examples.

The work is composed for choir and organ, and in nearly all 50 presentations of the motto it is played by the organ, sometimes by the organ alone, sometimes in unison or octave with one or more choir parts, sometimes the choir parts have something different from the organ. There is only one instance of the motto being presented by the choir without the organ following it, the seven concluding bars of the *Credo*, where it is sung by the sopranos.

But the most important – and musically most challenging feature – is that Gounod over the 50 appearances lets the motto start on each of the seven degrees of the diatonic scale.

Starting tone:	c	d	e	f	g	a	h
Number of appearances:	11	13	3	8	7	7	1

c, d, f, g, a, are the most frequent while e and b appear only a few times.

Below are a number of musical examples demonstrating the spectrum of ways the motto is integrated in the musical context.

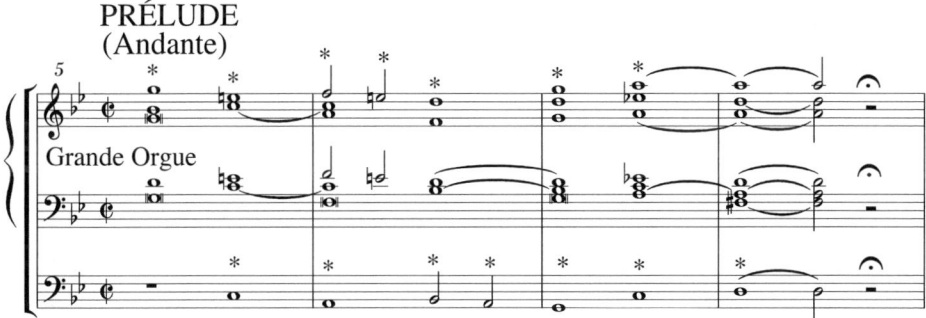

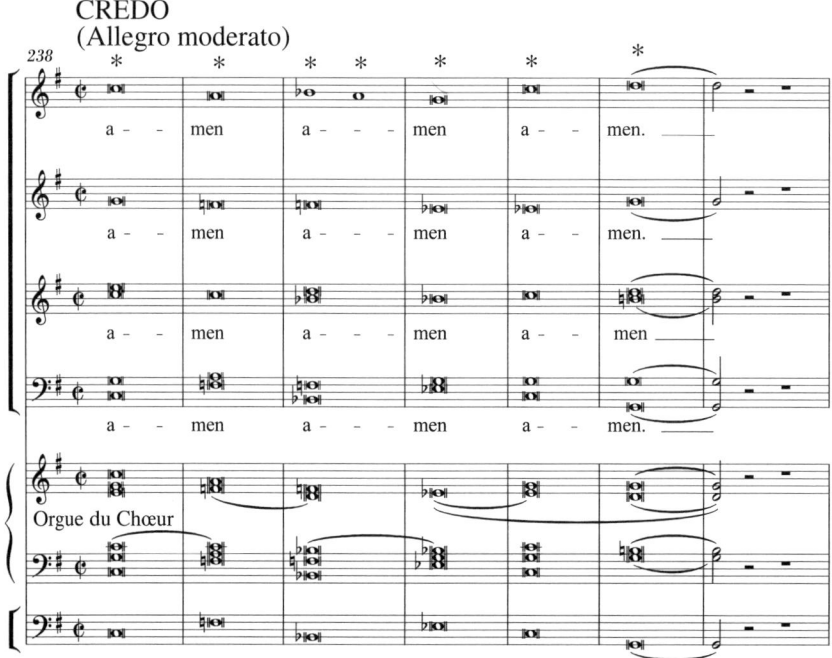

AGNUS DEI
(Moderato)

31

GLORIA
(Allegro moderato)

CREDO
(Allegro moderato)

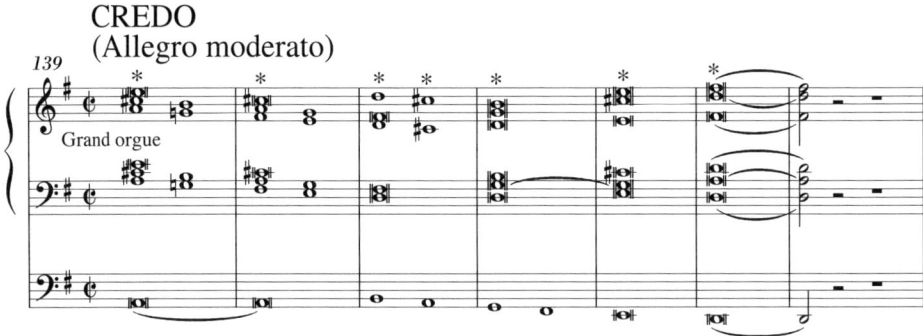

So much for the formal structure of Gounod's *Quatrième Messe Solennelle*, closely related to the *cantus firmus* masses of the past – but without exactly being one. Another mass which comes to mind is the very first 'modern' mass, Guillaume de Machaut's *Messe de Nostre Dame*. In this epoch-making work Machaut creates musical unity between the movements by letting a motto appear in all of them.

A method very much like that which Gounod applies in his *Quatrième Messe Solennelle*. Gounod's application of the *Credo* intonation, however, is far more comprehensive and radical.

Summa summarum, Gounod applies in *Quatrième Messe Solennelle* a structural principle so retrospective that I don't hesitate to label it retro-Renaissance.

Also the work's immediate stylistic appearance is decidedly retrospective. In passages the style is almost purely Palestrinian albeit that baroque-infected style which Johann Joseph Fux taught in *Gradus ad Parnassum* (1725) – in contrast to Knud Jeppesen's genuine Palestrinastyle.

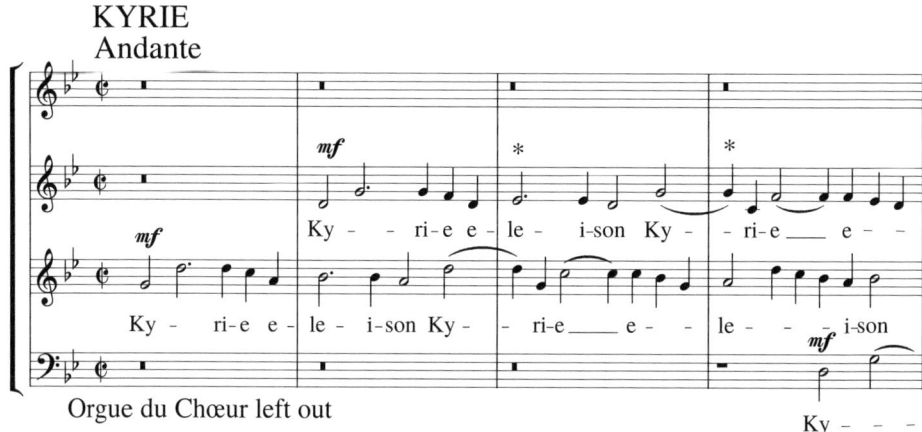

The dissonances marked with * do not belong to the vocabulary of the Renaissance.

Passages in this Fux-infected style appear frequently in Gounod's *Quatrième Messe Solennelle*.

But there are also passages in a more recent style. Thus the concluding *Hosanna* in the *Sanctus*-movement is set to a fugue with a modern tonal disposition of *dux* and *comes*:

BENEDICTUS

Orgue du Chœur left out

The musical style of the choir's part in *Quatrième Messe Solennelle* oscillates between what you might label pseudo-Palestrinian style and almost pure baroque style, both retrospective musical ways of expression.

A few concluding words about the organ-part or rather the organ-parts. The work is scored for two organs, an Orgue du Chœur, which largely follows the choir, and a Grand Orgue, that takes care of the individual preludes and interludes, which are more freely composed than the choir parts. In those one may even come across chromatic passages, something absent in the choir.

But apart from these isolated and brief strains of romanticism the *Quatrième Messe Solenelle* is in every respect retrospective by way of musical expression.

Messe No. 5 aux séminaires in C major (1871)[35]

This is a missa brevis (*in casu* a mass without the *Credo*). It is scored for a very small ensemble, three male soloists (TBB), a three-part male choir (TBB) and organ. Its musical style is very simple, mostly note-against-note harmonies and very few instances of imitation. Because of these limited demands on the musical forces the editor, Manfred Frank, believes that this mass – and others like it – was intended for liturgical use. However, the subtitle 'aux séminaires' suggests that it might also have had an educational function.

A few music examples will suffice to illustrate the musical style of this composition:

---

35. Charles Gounod: *Messe No. 5 aux séminaires* in C major.

KYRIE
(Moderato)

Since there is very little expressiveness in the music and nothing that goes beyond the rules of cadential harmony we may safely label its style as retro-classicistic

Messe de Requiem in C major[36]

This work, Gounod's last (arranged and edited by Henri Busser (1895)), is classical-romantic with an inclination towards the romantic.

The first movement consists of *Introitus* and *Kyrie* together. The time signature is 12/8 realized in a way that might as well have been notated as 4/4 with quaver triplets as the most prominent note value. The work opens with a descending chromatic line in flute 2 and clarinet 2 with flute 1 and clarinet 1 staying on the starting note, a musical figure ending on a sustained tritone. This figure is repeated an octave higher. A dull pizzicato accompaniment in the strings heralds the entry of the choir with the words *Requiem aeternam dona eis Domine, et lux perpetua luceat eis*. After 26 bars, the prominent characteristic of which is that it is written in two parts with a chromatic ascending melodic line, comes the verse, *Te decet hymnus*, in four-part harmony over a pedal point on c. The 29 bars of the verse pass directly into the *Kyrie*, the nine

---

36. Charles Gounod: *Requiem* in C major, op. posth.

exclamations of which form a descending chromatic line in the soprano over an intense series of chords:

Graduale *Requiem aeternam dona eis Domine* is left out in this Requiem.
Tractus *Absolve me Domine* is left out in this Requiem.

The Sequence *Dies irae*

The Sequence is the longest of the movements. With 52 of the score's 111 pages the Sequence is almost half the total length of the work.

The text of the Sequence, *Dies irae*, invites to a highly dramatic interpretation; but as far as musical drama goes Gounod's Requiem is relatively moderate. The movement oscillates between slightly dramatic passages and more lyrical passages with soft and plain melodic lines.

Mors stupebit is an example of the first:

SÉQUENCE
(Allegro moderato)

One of the finest examples of the lyrical passages is *Recordare*, where the lyrical melody – maybe a little sentimental – is presented first by a soprano soloist and then repeated by the choir in four-part, homophonic harmony.

This melody is repeated *in extenso* to the closing verse: *Huic ergo parce Deus. Pie Jesu Domine, Dona eis requiem.*

The Offertory *Domine Jesu Christe* is absent.

Sanctus

The opening Sanctus is short, largely with the organ alone in the accompaniment. It is homophonic in almost pure cadential harmony all the way to *Benedictus*, which here – as normally – is given its own movement: *Andante quasi religioso*, with a gentle vocal duet, soprano and tenor. The text, *Benedictus qui venit in nomine Domine,* is also presented by the choir in its own individual setting. The concluding *Hosanna* is even more Spartan than the first time we heard it.

After the *Sanctus* Gounod has inserted a movement with the text *Pie Jesu Domine, dona eis requiem sempiternam. Amen,* designated as a: "Variante pour l'élévation, au lieu de Benedictus," as we find it with several other French composers.

Agnus Dei and Communio

After an eight bar instrumental introduction follows the threefold *Agnus Dei, qui tollis peccata mundi: dona eis requiem,* shaped as a huge sequence-like structure:

Agnus 1: 6 bars, opening note in soprano, a
Interlude 1: 4 bars, opening note in vl.1, b flat
Agnus 2: 6 bars, opening note in soprano, b
Interlude 2: 4 bars, opening note in vl.1, c
Agnus 3: 6 bars, opening note in soprano, c sharp
Interlude 3: 4 bars, opening note in vl.1, a

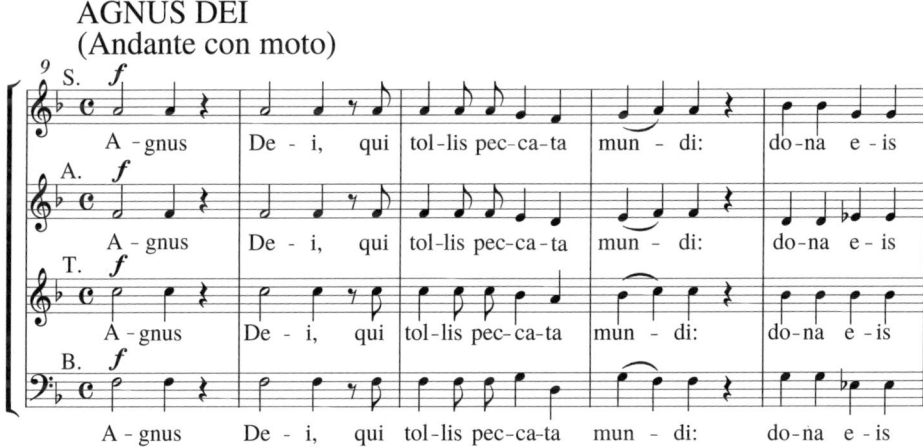

The concluding *Agnus Dei: dona eis requiem sempiternam* forms the definitive F major cadence of the *Agnus Dei* movement. It passes directly into the *Communio, Lux aeterna*, consisting of 24 discrete, homophonic bars in the choir followed by 21 concluding bars bringing the *Recordare* melody in purely instrumental guise and the final C major cadences over a pedal on c.

2.3 Other Vocal Works

The Seven Words of Our Saviour upon the Cross (1858)[37]

This cantata is written for four part mixed choir throughout, except for the seventh word, which is scored for two choirs much like the polychoral style of the Venetian school. Note-against-note chords in pre-cadential harmonic style is the prevailing texture:

---

37. Charles Gounod: *The Seven Words of Our Saviour Upon the Cross.*

At the other end of the stylistic spectrum we find the following, chromatic madrigalism:

Without doubt a retrospective musical way of expression.

Mors et Vita, Gallia, La Rédemption

The following works *Mors et Vita* (1885)[38], *Gallia* (1871)[39] and *La Rédemption* (1882)[40] unfold throughout within the classical-romantic style domaine.

---

38. Charles Gounod: *Mors et Vita, A Sacred Trilogy*, Vocal Score with Pianoforte Accompaniment.
39. Charles Gounod: *Gallia*, Lamentation.
40. Charles Gounod: *La Rédemption, Trilogie Sacrée*.

Mors et vita, a sacred trilogy dedicated to Pope Leo XIII, was produced for the first time in Birmingham at the Festival of 1885. This work is divided into three parts, *Mors, Judicium, Vita*. The first consists of a *Requiem*, the second depicts *The Judgment*, the third *Eternal Life*.

Charles Gounod in the preface to the piano-score: "Among the musical figures that go through the whole work and the easiest to perceive, I shall first and foremost direct my attention to the following:

which expresses the fear caused by the mere idea of legal action, followed by fear of chastisement.

Ascending or descending the application of that figure makes up a sequence of three major seconds, together a tritone, whose tough expression is rediscovered in the passing of the sentence of divine justice, the suffering of the condemned, and which throughout the work is combined with figures expressing totally different feelings, such as those in the 'Sanctus' and the 'Pie Jesu' in the requiem, which make up the first section [of the work].

This second figure, that of sadness and tears, becomes by the application of the major key and the change of a simple note the figure of comfort and joy.

and expresses the happiness of the blessed.

Finally the following figure –

the triple superposition of which form the framework of the augmented fifth, and announces the resurrection of the dead through the terrifying fanfare sounding from the angelic trumpet of which St. Paul speaks in one of his letters to the Corinthians."[41]

Like *Mors et Vita La Rédemption* is a cantata trilogy, while *Gallia* is a lamentation motet.

---

41. Original French text: "Parmi les formes musicales dont la persistance à travers l'œuvre est le plus saisissable, j'appellerai principalement l'attention sur celles qui suivent:–
[Music example]
exprimant la terreur qu'inspire le sentiment de la Justice seule, et par suite l'angoisse du châtiment. Cette forme, dont l'emploi soit ascendant soit descendant, présente une suite de trois secondes majeures, donne un total de quarte augmentée dont l'expression farouche se retrouve dans les arrêts de la Justice divine, dans les souffrances des damnés, et se combine, dans tout l'ouvrage, avec les formes qui expriment des sentiments tout différents, comme dans le 'Sanctus' et le 'Pie Jesu' du Requiem, qui compose la première partie.
[Music example]
[Music example]
Cette seconde forme, celle des tristesses et des larmes, devient, par l'emploi du mode majeur et l'altération d'une simple note, la forme des consolations et des joies:
[Music example]
exprime la félicité des bienheureux.
Enfin, la forme suivante –
[Music example]
par sa triple superposition qui donne un cadre de quinte augmentée, annonce le réveil des morts par cette effrayante fanfare de la trompette angélique dont parle St. Paul dans l'une de ses épîtres aux Corinthiens."

3. Camille Saint-Saëns (1835-1921)

Camille Saint-Saëns was recognized as an infant prodigy gifted with absolute pitch, a composer from the age of three and an incredibly talented pianist. At his official debut concert he played piano concertos by Mozart and Beethoven at the age of 10.

He entered the Paris Conservatoire in 1848 and over the following decades his reputation grew steadily both as a composer and a pianist.

Following several unhappy incidents in his private life, he turned into a lonely nomad, and over the last 30 years of his life he travelled ceaselessly, mostly to Algeria and Egypt.

However, his creative power remained unabated until his death in 1921.

3.1 The Symphonic Works

From Saint-Saëns' enormous and varied musical production we shall look at his Symphonies to start with.

There are five symphonies in total.

Apart from the scores the main source for my study of Saint-Saëns' symphonies is Daniel Martin Fallon's dissertation.[42]

Saint-Saëns' first step into the symphonic genre was taken in 1850, when he, at the age of 15, composed a symphony in A major. The symphony shows influence from Mozart, Beethoven and others and must be regarded as an exercise with which I shall not occupy myself further.

Symphony No.1

Three years later Saint-Saëns wrote his *Symphony No. 1* in E flat major during the summer of 1853.[43] It has four movements with the *Adagio* in the third position.

---

42. Daniel Martin Fallon: *The Symphonies and Symphonic Poems of Camille Saint-Saëns* (Hereafter *Daniel Fallon*).
43. Camille Saint-Saëns: *Symphony No. 1* in E flat major.

The symphony's route to performance is bizarre to say the least. Saint-Saëns submitted it to Mr. Seghers of the committee of the Société Sainte-Cécile in 1853. Seghers – to whom the symphony is dedicated – was in favour of having it performed, but he doubted whether the governing committee would agree, so he passed it on to the committee, pretending it had been created by an anonymous German composer. However, the trick worked and the symphony was enthusiastically accepted and given its first performance on December 18th, 1853.

The first movement is a sonata form with a very short, slow introduction which reappears at important structural locations in the *Allegro* section: at bar 93, the beginning of the Development section, and at bar 200, the beginning of the Recapitulation:

The main theme is derived from the slow introduction.

It is repeated by clarinet 1 and followed by a bridge passage, which leads to the second theme in the third-related key of C major in bar 59.

The second theme is made up of several motives, marked with brackets in the music example below:

The ensuing bridge passage borrows heavily from especially the end of the second theme. It ends up in bar 93 with the reappearance of the slow introduction, here in a much lighter instrumentation.

Apart from the reappearance of the slow introduction in bars 93 and 200 (here scored for full orchestra, fortissimo), the Development section, the Recapitulation and the Coda, which enters at bar 256, have nothing particularly interesting to offer.

Certainly a classical-romantic movement, with several references to the classical masters. Or as Daniel Martin Fallon puts it: "In reviewing the movement as a whole, one is struck by Saint-Saëns' acceptance of Beethoven – or perhaps Beethoven via Schumann – as his model."[44]

The second movement is a march-scherzo in G major. But apart from the time-signature there is nothing martial whatsoever about this delicate movement, which – like the opening movement – plays on sudden modulations to third-related keys.

The first theme, which reappears several times, is a delicate legato melody in G major played by the oboe with a light accompaniment in the strings.

Several other themes and motives crop up in passages some of which display tendencies to musical development. However, this movement does not fall into any specific formal category. It may be perceived as a kind of rondo, as does Daniel Martin Fallon: "This reappearance of the main theme in the tonic suggests that the movement is organized in rondo fashion, and, although

---

44. *Daniel Fallon*: p. 96.

this is not literally the case, the constant recurrence of this theme in the tonic indicates that varied repetition is prominent throughout."⁴⁵

Again a classical-romantic way of expression. Definitely more classical than romantic.

The third movement is a lyrical *Adagio* in E major, the most romantic part of the symphony. Daniel Martin Fallon writes about it: "The lyrical Adagio which follows is an expansive movement in abridged sonata form scored for a full orchestra. In this movement, with its heavy texture and rich harmonic palette, Saint-Saëns has created a work of great seriousness and gravity, which contrasts with the preceding Marche-Scherzo. This movement is an imposing undertaking and indicates Saint-Saëns' interest in the Germanic avant-garde with Schumann at its head."⁴⁶

The finale consists of three parts, the first of which is structured as the Exposition section of a sonata form with main theme, second theme, bridge passages etc. The main theme group consists of two themes

---

45. *Daniel Fallon*: p. 99.
46. *Daniel Fallon*: p.104.

The second theme is presented bar 68:

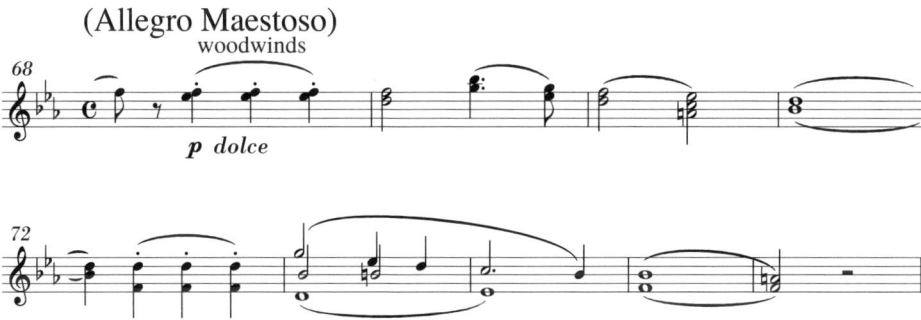

The second part of the Finale is a fugue based on the following subject:

The third is a stretto prolongation of the fugue which sets in bar 192 after a fermata and functions as a Coda.

If you consider the fugue to function as the Development section, the whole movement may be described as a sonata form without Recapitulation.

Its general way of musical expression is definitely classical-romantic with a tendency to romantic gigantism, which is, however, counterbalanced by its short playing time (between seven and eight minutes) and the extensive use of fugal elements.

Symphony in F major (URBS ROMA)

In 1856 Saint-Saëns submitted a symphony in F major[47] to a composition contest announced and sponsored by the Société-Cécile of Bordeaux. It was submitted under the motto *Urbs Roma* – for which the reason, if any, is unknown to me. Saint-Saëns' symphony won the first prize. It was written hastily between the 2nd and 25th of July, i.e. a few months before his 21st birthday anniversary. It was premièred June 10th 1857 with Saint-Saëns as conductor.

The first movement is a sonata-form opening with a majestic motto, rhythmically distinctive and brought out by the horns. "This is followed immediately [bar 5] by a passage which resembles the symphonic introductions of Haydn and Beethoven except that Saint-Saëns' harmonic palette is more colourful."[48] The slow introduction leads via a crescendo to the *Allegro 6/4* presenting the 13 bar first theme of the Exposition section (bar 22). Then follows a rather independent development-like bridge passage which leads to the second theme in A flat major in bar 71. The second theme is presented several times in various keys (C major, e minor) and a decrescendo leads to the repetition of the Exposition section in bar 141.

Opening with a D flat major chord the Development section modulates through various keys and displays several variations of the main theme. Bar 210 a scale-like motif is introduced. In bar 222 it is used as the subject of a short fuga or fugato, and finally the opening motto from the slow introduction appears twice in C major (bars 235 and 243). The scale-like motif continues, both between the two presentations of the opening motto and after, until the Recapitulation comes in at bar 261. The Recapitulation is shorter than the Exposition section, mainly because most of the bridge passage is omitted. The Recapitulation stays in F major according to the laws of the sonata form. In bar 364 comes a short *Largo*, once again presenting the opening motto. In the Coda (bar 368) the main theme is heard for the last time.

---

47. Camille Saint-Saëns: *Symphony, Urbs Roma* in F major, (1856).
48. *Daniel Fallon*: p. 135.

The second movement is a Scherzo in a minor with Trio in A major and Coda. The Scherzo section presents two themes, the first being a rather robust one in a minor:

This theme is presented four times alternating with various bridge passages. Then comes an extended second theme in e minor:

After a further 14 bars a short, rushing scale passage leads to yet another repetition of the first theme followed by a new bridge passage that brings us to the Trio.

The trio section in A major is built on mainly two musical ideas, a scale-like theme (or motif) in parallel thirds (predominant note value the quaver) and descending and ascending chromatic scales (predominant note value crotchet). Towards the end the key changes to a minor to provide a smooth transition to the repetition of the Scherzo section.

At the end of the Trio Saint-Saëns indicates that both the Scherzo section and the Trio are to be repeated.[49] The relatively long Coda is a varied repetition of the Scherzo section, however, without the second theme, and in the end infiltrated by trio material. The whole movement then exhibits a five-section grand form:

Scherzo / Trio / Scherzo / Trio / Scherzo-varied, a form often used by the Danish composer Niels W. Gade in his Scherzi.

The slow movement falls in five sections. The first section opens with a four bar theme in f minor, *Moderato, assai serioso*, time signature **c**:

It consists of two motives, the first of which comprises bars 1-3. The other is the somewhat 'spooky' descending chromatic line bar 4.

The second section displays a great contrast to the first section. The key is F major and it presents a graceful melodic line consisting of two subphrases:

---

49. Saint-Saëns' note: "N.B. Si riprende dal segno tutto il minore [= the scherzo section] e ancora una volta tutto il maggiore [= the trio], dopo quella si eseguita la Coda".

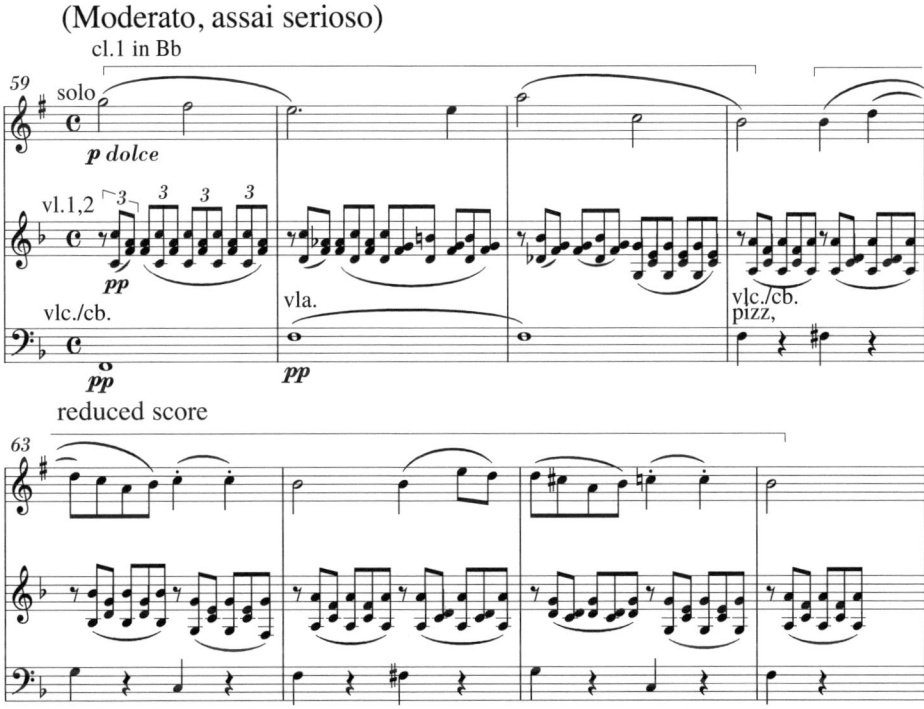

The third section returns to f minor and the opening theme, which is now subject to a development-like treatment scented with the second subphrase from the second section.

Section four is in C major and presents the same material as section 2; but where the predominant accompaniment moves in quaver triplets in section 2, it moves in semiquavers in section four. A bridge passage based on the second subphrase of the second section leads to the concluding section five in which we return to f minor and the musical motives of section one.

The Finale is a theme with seven variations. The key is F major and the time signature 3/4. The theme consists of two repeated sections, the first, however, is written out because of slight differences between the two presentations:

The first section is made up of two four bar periods. The second consists of three four bar periods. The harmonic frame-work is easily perceived.

Basically the variations in the finale of the *Urbs Roma Symphony* are figural variations with elements of character variation already present in the classical variation form.

The six variations:

Variation 1: The theme easily recognized, key and harmony unaltered. Semiquavers added to the melody, but not so many that it makes recognition of the theme difficult.

Variation 2: Time signature changed to 9/8 (i.e. as if the quavers of the theme are replaced by quaver triplets). This variation is slightly prolonged.

Variation 3: Tempo changed to *Meno Mosso* and the melodic variation somewhat more radical than in the preceding variations.

Variation 4: L'istesso tempo, key f minor and the rhythm as in the revolutionary march in the Finale of Beethoven's *Eroica Symphony*, but it sounds much less threatening in Saint-Saëns' version. The variation is prolonged with a tail leading to

Variation 5 in 5/4 with dotted bar-lines subdividing it into 2+3/4. This variation comprises the first part of the theme only.

Variation 6: Time signature 3/4 *Andante con moto*. The concluding variation continues into a Coda which might be counted as a self-contained variation 7.

As a whole the *Urbs Roma Symphony* is a classical-romantic composition.

Symphony No. 2

The manuscript, printer's copy to Saint-Saëns' *Symphony No. 2 in a minor* op. 55 is dated September 1859. The symphony, however, was not published until 1878.[50]

It has four movements. The second one is the slow movement.

According to Daniel Martin Fallon the first movement is based on a 'non-programmatic idée fixe' which shows itself in various arrays in the rather long introduction:

---

50. Camille Saint-Saëns: *Symphony No. 2 in a minor op. 55*.

The introduction alternates between *Allegro marcato* 6/4 (𝅗𝅥. = 69) and *Più Allegro*.

The Exposition opens with a fugue using the *idée fixe* as subject (bar 66). With bar 128 comes the sonata form's second theme in F major:

The short Development section (bar 156) begins with a variation of the second theme (bar 158), and in bar 206 the revised and intensified Recapitulation sets in.

The application of the 'non-programmatic idée fixe' endows this movement with a marked feeling of austerity.

The slow movement contrasts strongly with the first movement. It is light and graceful, with a thin orchestration and it is short. It displays three themes which unfold as follows:

A A' B A" C C' Coda

Theme A is in E major:

Theme A is repeated in a different orchestration, A'.
Theme B in c sharp minor:

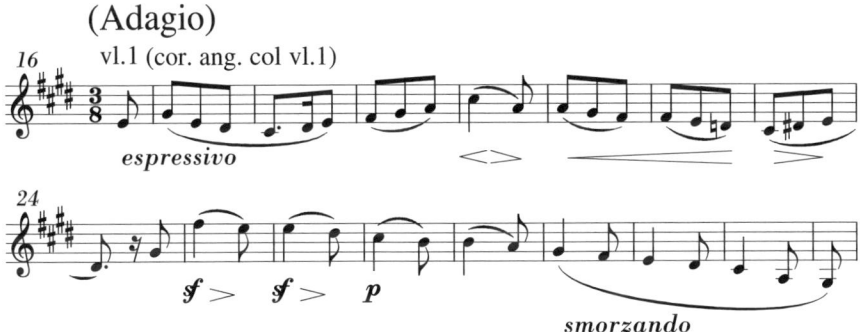

A few bars of transition lead bar 36 to the reappearance of A in a new instrumentation, A"; theme C enters in bar 44. Theme C is derived from the conclusion of theme A

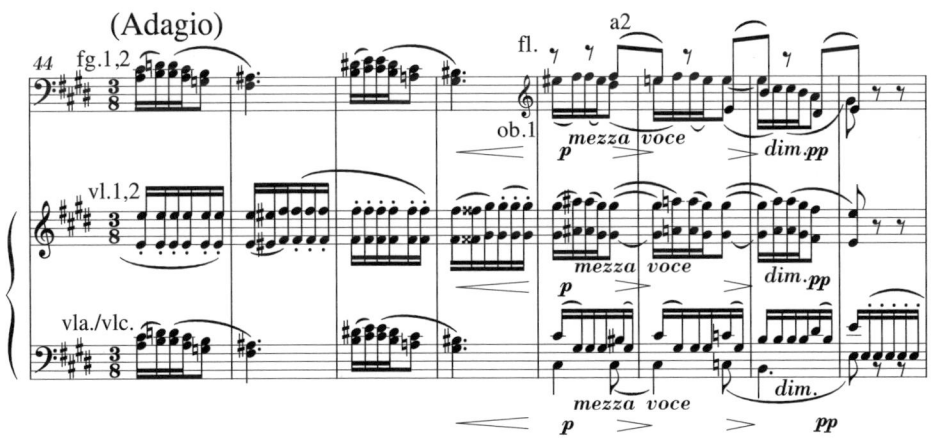

Theme C is also repeated and rescored, C', and finally the Coda enters at bar 60.

Even this theme is repeated before the movement comes to an end with the two last bars of A forming its final cadence.

The third movement is a Scherzo in a minor with a Trio in A major. There is no repetition of the 202 bars of the Scherzo section after the trio, merely 81 bars presenting material from the scherzo section as well as from the trio. Certainly a very singular formal disposition.

The Scherzo section is built on several motives and displays generally a robust character, whereas the Trio section is more lightly scored, and built on a single syncopated melodic idea, which brings to mind the Scherzo from Beethoven's *Pastoral Symphony*, the Scherzo from his *String Quartet* in F major op. 135 and the Scherzo from Niels W. Gade's *String Quintet* in e minor op. 8.

The Finale, *Prestissimo* 6/8, opens in A major with a theme much like that of the finale of Mendelssohn's *Italian Symphony*. Theme 1:

Several other themes or motives are added in the subsequent bars. Theme 2:

This may be interpreted as a variation of the *idée fixe* from the first movement

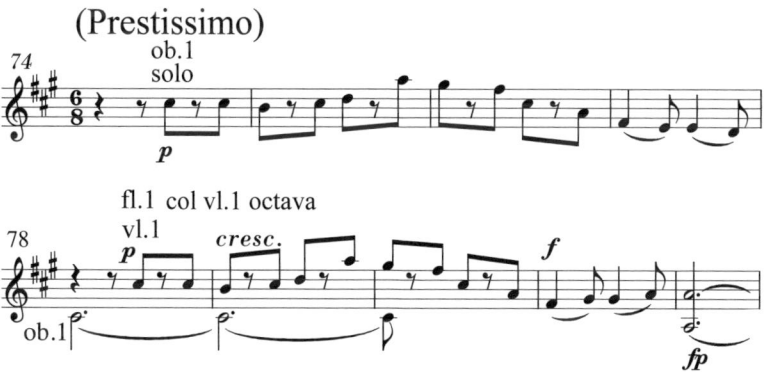

Bar 107 a theme from the scherzo is introduced:

Hereafter (bar 133) theme 1 reappears; but is this the repetition of the Exposition section or is it the Development section of the sonata form? Theme 2 follows bar 170, but from bar 190 proper developmental work begins. It

goes on until bar 349, where the introduction of theme 1 marks the beginning of the shortened Recapitulation, only themes 1, 2 and the theme from the scherzo are given. With bar 448 comes the Coda, which – after one more presentation of theme 1 introduces a quotation from the end of the Adagio. The finale ends with the Scherzo theme combined with theme 1 followed by concluding cadences.

If this symphony is not dominated by retro-classicistic transparency, it is even less romantic by way of musical expression. The individual movements are all connected with classical models, but Saint-Saëns twists the models rather radically and mixes them with his own ideas. Its shortness and seriousness yet not romantic way of expression make it an antiromantic work. However, by combining elements from all four movements in the finale, Saint-Saëns' Symphony in a minor also represents an ambitious attempt to create a symphonic apotheosis. And this is definitely a romantic endeavour.

Organ Symphony

Saint-Saëns' last symphony is the so-called *Organ Symphony* in c minor op. 78[51], created in 1886.

The orchestra is large, 3 flutes, 2 oboes and English horn, 2 clarinets and bass-clarinet, 2 bassoons and doublebassoon, 4 French horns, 3 trumpets, 3 trombones and tuba, timpani, organ and strings.

I shall not say much about the Organ symphony here. It is classical-romantic in its way of musical expression, with such an emphasis on its romantic aspect that one might be tempted to label it new-German without programmatic contents, that is, if such a characterization would not be a contradiction in terms.

Orchestral Suite op. 49[52]

This work (1862-63) needs attention, not because it is a symphony, which it is not; but because it has been referred to as a symphony in various catalogues and inventories, some of which refer to both a D major Symphony and a D major orchestral suite. Octave Séré lists them as follows:

"Symphony in D-major, 1859. Unpublished.

---

51. Camille Saint-Saëns: *Symphony No.3, Organ Symphony* in c minor op. 78.
52. Camille Saint-Saëns: *Suite pour Orchestre* op. 49.

Suite for Orchestra: 1. Prelude; 2. Sarabande; 3. Gavotte; 4. Romance; 5 Finale, 1863. Paris, Durand, 1877."53

Daniel Martin Fallon's investigation leads to the following conclusion: "There is no evidence to suggest that Saint-Saëns himself ever considered the suite a 'symphony.' The Suite for Orchestra is among the composer's 'neo-classic' works which incorporate eighteenth-century dance forms."54 The five movements of the *Orchestral Suite* are: No.1 Prélude, No. 2. Sarabande, No. 3 Gavotte, No. 4. Romance, No. 5 Final.

The orchestra: two flutes, two oboes (also English horn), two clarinets, two bassoons, two French horns, two trumpets, timpani and strings.

The static character of this movement is brought about by the canonic structure of the music and the use of long pedals in the low intruments throughout the prelude.

---

53. Octave Séré: *Musiciens Français d'Aujourd'hui*, pp. 378f. Quoted from *Daniel Fallon*: p. 198.
54. *Daniel Fallon*: p. 199.

No. 2, SARABANDE

The Sarabande alternates between homophonic passages rendering the basic Sarabande rhythm and more fluent passages played sometimes alone, sometimes together with the Sarabande rhythm.

No. 3, GAVOTTE

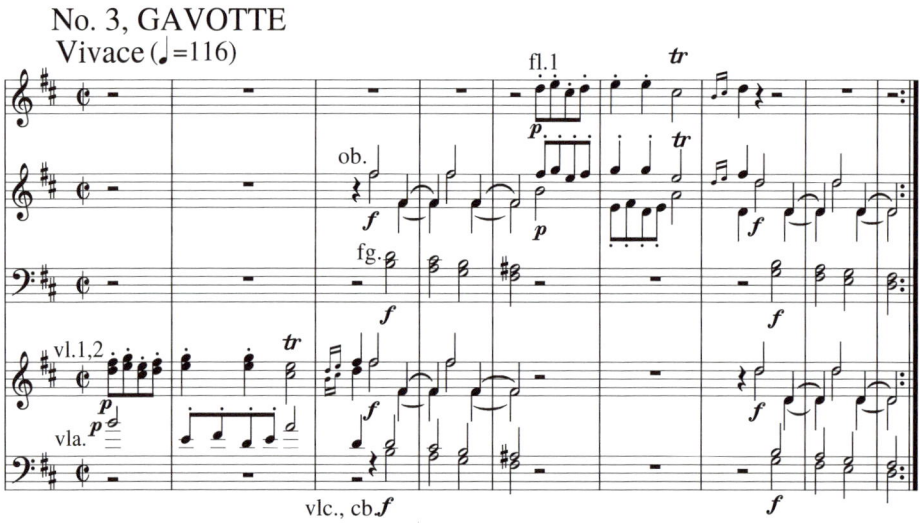

A Gavotte with Trio, the Gavotte section in b minor, the Trio in B major. The Gavotte section is dominated by symmetrical two-bar periods with clear-cut rhythm, the Trio is scored for two flutes over a pedal on b'' and b' in the violins.

The Romance is the only expressive movement of op. 49, and also the longest (playing time about 6 minutes). Still, it is very transparent and the development of the themes easy to follow.

No. 5: Finale, *Allegro vivace*.

This movement is a classical *Kehraus* finale with rushing semiquavers from first to last.

To conclude: There is hardly one single bar in op. 49 which could not have been written by one of the Viennese classical masters, and I do not hesitate to label Saint-Saëns' *Orchestral Suite* a retro-classicistic work.

3.2 Piano Music

Piano Concertos

Saint-Saëns wrote five piano concertos over the period 1858-1896.

The first (D major op. 17)[55] in 1858.
The second (g minor op. 22)[56] in 1868.
The third (E flat major op. 29)[57] in 1869.
The fourth (C major op. 44)[58] in 1875.
The fifth (F major op. 102)[59] in 1896.

They are all written in classical-romantic style, with a general tendency to unfold in the romantic end of the spectrum, a fact probably connected with Saint-Saëns' complete mastery of the romantic virtuoso / equilibristic piano style, to which he gave free rein in these fourteen movements with very few traces of retro-classicism. Here are a few comments on three selected movements:

Due to the beginning of the second movement of the first concerto one would expect this movement to develop into a full-blown Bach-pastiche but instead we get some really expressive, romantic passages in the piano, and Bach only returns once (bar 23) in this movement, which is otherwise dominated by the romantic piano passages.

The second movement of the second concerto is a Scherzo with no marked subdivision in Scherzo and Trio sections. It opens with a typical Scherzo theme (S). A contrasting, more *cantabile* and a little vulgar melody (bar 75) may reasonably be perceived as a Trio section (T). The movement is laid out as follows:

S_1	T_1	S_2	T_2	S_3	T_3	S_4
bar 1	75	131	185	199	257	309

A very unusual structure of four Scherzo sections and three Trio sections of very different lengths. The most singular characteristic of this Scherzo is, in

---

55. Camille Saint-Saëns: *Concerto No. 1* for Piano and Orchestra, op. 17.
56. Camille Saint-Saëns: *Concerto No. 2* for Piano and Orchestra, op. 22.
57. Camille Saint-Saëns: *Concerto No. 3* for Piano and Orchestra, op. 29.
58. Camille Saint-Saëns: *Concerto No. 4* for Piano and Orchestra, op. 44.
59. Camille Saint-Saëns: *Concerto No. 5* for Piano and Orchestra, op. 103.

my opinion, the subtle moderations of the basic tempo marked *tranquillo* (bars 87, 157 and 269) – an extremely humoristic idea.

The third movement I shall lay stress on is the first movement of the fourth concerto. It is really two movements, an *Allegro moderato* and an *Andante*.

The *Allegro moderato* is a theme with variations. The theme itself is presented by the strings. It is built up of two eight-bar phrases, each of which is immediately repeated and varied by the piano.

Then comes the formal first variation, still presented by the strings and still with varied repetitions of its two phases in the piano. This structure, which we might call a double variation, continues to the end of the *Allegro moderato*.

The ensuing *Andante* might be labelled a *choral variation*, and together with the preceding *Allegro moderato* it forms one huge triple variation movement. The choral grows out of the orchestral accompaniment over a piano line in very short note values. The first phrase of the choral melody's four phrases emerges in bar 14 in the woodwinds, the others follow in bars 17, 20 and 22. From then on, the choral melody is presented in different guises, in four-part harmony, as a single melodic line, alone or interwoven with virtuoso piano passages.

Études for Piano

We shall take a brief look at the three times six études for piano:

Op. 52,[60] (1868, 1877) and op. 111,[61] (1892, 1899) each contain six études for piano two hands.

In the booklet to Mi-Joo Lee's recording Ulrich Mahlert writes about op. 52 and op. 111[62]: "The op. 52 and op. 111 études occupy the generic-historical middle ground between the great études of Chopin and Liszt, works already recognized as classics, and the twelve extremely novel études composed by Debussy in 1915. While Chopin features intricate, tightly woven piano parts and Liszt a monumental alfresco style of rich contrasts, Saint-Saëns has a smoother, broader, and entirely more pleasant style to offer. In other words, he may be said to have moderated the eccentricities of his two

---

60. Camille Saint-Saëns: *Six Études pour Piano, 1er Livre* op. 52.
61. Camille Saint-Saëns: *Six Études pour Piano, Deuxième Livre* op. 111.
62. Musikproduktion Dabringhaus und Grimm, MDG 604 0590-2: Camille Saint-Saëns: *Etudes op. 52, 111, Album pour Piano op. 72* with Mi-Joo Lee, Piano. Liner notes by Ulrich Mahlert, 1995.

immediate predecessors Chopin and Liszt with a Mendelssohnian classicism. This does not mean that our composer's études are any less sparkling. To the contrary, his mostly slenderer piano parts open the way for a racing facility involving the most varied forms and verging on break-neck speed. On numerous occasions the demands he places on the pianist even go beyond what Chopin and Liszt call for in their études. The Étude op. 52, no. 2, offers an especially fine example of this. Here the requirement of finger independence is developed in unusual fashion: the pianist has to emphasize different tones in the repeating chords and then to form melodic contours from them. Debussy seems to have drawn on and developed many a novel playing model from our composer's études. A number of different relations exist between the chromatic (Saint-Saëns op. 111, no. 2; Debussy: No. 7) and third-interval (Saint-Saëns: op. 111, nos. 1 and 5; Debussy: No. 2) études of the two. Saint-Saëns expanded the playing tasks in his études not only through piano-part innovations but also with retrospective reference to the music of past centuries. Here we are referring to the fugues in the three *Prélude et Fugue* pairs (op. 52, nos. 3 and 5; op. 111, no. 3). In these works Saint-Saëns was practising a 'strict style' oriented to that of J.S. Bach – as Muzio Clementi had done in his *Gradus ad Parnassum* étude collection."

Prélude et Fugue op. 52 No. 3: The prelude moves in fast semiquaver triplets from first to last, not unlike the c minor prelude from Bach's *Well-tempered Clavier* volume 1, and the fugue also comes close to its model.

The preludes of op. 52 No. 5 and op. 111 No. 3 are more like classical-romantic character pieces, whereas the fugues are as Bach-like as that of op. 52 No. 3.

To conclude: The three fugues in op. 52 and 111 may safely be characterized as retro-classicistic or rather retro-baroque compositions. As to the preludes I dare only characterize that of op. 52 No. 3 as such.

Les Cloches de Las Palmas (op. 111 No. 4) displays some impressionistic traits.

The *Six études for the left hand alone* op. 135 from 1912 stand a little by themselves.[63] They appear more objective – in another word more 'dry'– than op. 52 and 111. As a whole op. 135 is formed as a suite or partita or sonata da camera in contemporary terminology: Prélude, Alla Fuga, Moto Perpetuo, Bourrée, Élégie, Gigue.

---

63. Camille Saint-Saëns: *Six Études pour la main gauche seule* op. 135.

There are few markings of expression and indications of change of tempo – most in the Élégie.

The suite form and the generally objective (= non-expressive) style are retrospective traits allowing us to classify op. 135 as a retro-classicistic work.

3.3 The Chamber Music

The string quartets

Saint-Saëns wrote two string quartets, both relatively late in his career, the first one in e minor op. 112, 1899, the other in G major op. 153, 1918.[64]

Of the two I find op. 153 the more interesting. It opens with a transparent *Allegro animato* which reminds one of Mozart or rather Haydn but a closer look at the harmonic language reveals passages like the following (bar 207):

---

64. Camille Saint-Saëns: *Quartet for 2 violins, Viola and Cello*, op. 112, *Quartet No. 2 for 2 Violins, Viola and Cello*, op. 153.

Harmonic clashes like this are not found in either classical cadential harmony or romantic harmony. It would be necessary to go to a neo-classicist composer to encounter such harmonic structures but after all, we are in 1918.

The second movement, *Adagio molto*, is romantic in its general way of musical expression. Its opening bars go like this:

Even if the harmonies do not transgress the bounderies of romantic harmony, they are certainly extremely expressive, and unlike the objective, even dry musical style typical of Saint-Saëns.

The finale, which has a short, slow introduction labelled Interlude, consists of a series of short contrasting sections. In this finale Saint-Saëns exploits the possibilities of the open strings of the quartet's intruments. The style of the music is light and humorous.

Piano trio in F major, op. 18, 1864[65]

Saint-Saëns wrote this piano trio when he was 28 years of age. It has the four movements normal for chamber music of the 19th century. The Scherzo is placed as the third movement. The musical style is classical-romantic.

The septet

Saint-Saëns' *Septuor* op. 65[66] (1879-80) is scored for a rather unusual group of instruments: 2 violins, viola, cello, double bass, trumpet and piano. The unusual ensemble is undoubtedly due to the fact that the work was written for a chamber music society named *La Trompette*, founded by Émile Lemoine in 1867. Sabina Teller Ratner, who wrote the booklet for a recording of the *Septet*[67] refers to it as a 'neo-classical' work and mentions in this connection its use of 17th-century dance forms. Using my proposed terminology 'neo-classical' should be replaced by 'retro-classicistic.' Unless, of course, she means that the *Septet* is a genuine neo-classical work in line with works by Les Six, Stravinsky and Paul Hindemith. Maybe she does, see p. 98 below.

The musical style of the *Septet* is objective, quite un-emotional. At the end of the account of the septet Teller Ratner writes: "The four movements, labelled *Préambule*, *Menuet*, *Intermède* and *Gavotte et Final*, reveal the classical proclivity of the composer."

---

65. Camille Saint-Saëns: *Trio No. 1 for piano, violin and cello* in F major op. 18.
66. Camille Saint-Saëns: *Septuor* op. 65.
67. Hyperion CDA6743 1/2: Works by Camille Saint-Saëns played by the Nash Ensemble. Liner notes by Sabina Teller Ratner, 2005.

Le Carnaval des Animaux

Le Carnaval des Animaux (1886)[68] is scored for flute, clarinet, 2 violins, viola, cello, double bass, 2 pianos, xylophone and harmonica. Because of its many extramusical references it seems meaningless to try to place it within the range of the classical-romantic style spectrum.

It is, however, meaningful to analyse it with a view to a truly neo-classicistic hallmark, that of musical humour (see below pp. 102-103).

Sonata No. 2 for cello and piano, F major, op. 123[69]

The 2nd cello sonata (1905) is an altogether classical-romantic composition, serious throughout, with weight and length attached to each of its four movements. The only movement in which one may perceive a little retro-baroque is the Scherzo con Variazioni, its variation 6 being a fugue.

The sonatas for oboe, clarinet, and bassoon with piano

Sonata for oboe and piano D major op. 166 (1921)[70]
Sonata for clarinet and piano E flat major op. 167 (1921)[71]
Sonata for bassoon and piano G major op. 168 (1921)[72]

Sabina Teller Ratner writes about these three late sonatas for oboe, clarinet and bassoon: "The distinctive timbre and versatility of each instrument are expertly displayed. The spare, evocative, classical lines, haunting melodies, and superb formal structures underline these beacons of the neoclassical movement."[73] Again, does she mean genuine neo-classical or retro-classical?

---

68. Camille Saint-Saëns: *Le Carnaval des Animaux*.
69. Camille Saint-Saëns: *Sonata No. 2 for cello and piano*, op.123.
70. Camille Saint-Saëns: *Sonata for Oboe and Piano*, op. 166.
71. Camille Saint-Saëns: *Sonata for Clarinet and Piano*, op. 167.
72. Camille Saint-Saëns: *Sonata for Bassoon and Piano*, op. 168.
73. Hyperion CDA6743 1/2: Works by Camille Saint-Saëns played by the Nash Ensemble. Liner notes by Sabina Teller Ratner, 2005.

4. Niels W. Gade (1817-1890)

Gade's life spanned almost exactly the same years as that of Charles Gounod, and their *œuvre* display many similarities, but also many differences. Gade started his musical career as a Danish national romantic composer. Two of his early compositions, the Concert Overture *Echoes of Ossian*, op. 1 and his *Symphony No. 1* in c minor op. 5 were extremely well received in Leipzig, and from 1843 to 1848 Gade lived in Leipzig, where he had a brilliant career at the side of Mendelssohn, both as a composer and as a conductor of the Gewandhaus concerts. During his stay in Leipzig he adopted the more polished international musical style of Mendelssohn and from about 1846-47, the time of his *Symphony No. 3* in a minor op. 15, his compositional style changed to the classical-romantic one, however, not without an occasional return to the national-romantic idiom of his younger days.

4.1 String Quartets Nos. 1 and 2

We shall start our examination of Niels W. Gade with a purely instrumental composition, the first movement *Allegro moderato* of Gade's *String Quartet No. 1* in D major op. 63.[74]

Practically all Gade's chamber music was published immediately after it was created, with the string quartets as a striking exception. Gade wrote three quartets, in f minor, e minor and D major plus a couple of *juvenilia*. Of these only the D major quartet was published before his death in 1890.

The genesis of the D major quartet is long and complicated. In 1887 Gade finished the draft of a string quartet in d minor in four movements. Apparently in February 1888 he set to work again to give the quartet a final polishing, in the course of which he decided to give it a new first movement. The new first movement is in D major, which radically altered the tonal plan of the quartet:

First movement, *Allegro moderato* in D major
Second movement, *Allegretto vivace, scherzando* in B flat major

---

74. Niels W. Gade: WORKS, Series II, Vol. 2, The String Quartets.

Third movement, *Andante poco lento* in F major
Finale, *Moderato sostenuto / Allegro con brio* in D major

In a letter of April 30th 1888, the existence of the quartet was announced to Breitkopf & Härtel, who immediately replied that they wished to publish it. However, the work did not appear until the beginning of 1890.

Gade did not, however, discard the original first movement but transposed it a whole tone up to e minor and reused it as the opening movement of his e minor quartet.

The new D major movement is a clear-cut, pastoral movement in 6/8 metre, and appears so classicistic that one of my Copenhagen colleagues found occasion to remark that he found Gade's D major quartet a fine work, its time of composition, however, totally wrong.

Let us take a closer look at the new D major movement:
Needless to say, it is cast in sonata-form. The first theme:

It is repeated, and after a short concluding 'tail', it appears once again as from the beginning, this time ending up in A major in bar 53 with the second theme, actually not very different from the first theme by way of general expression.

The rest of this *Allegro moderato* is as clear and balanced as its two themes. Its infallible allegiance to the classical virtues makes it a fine example of Gade's retro-classicistic style.

We shall now take a look at the e minor quartet (1877, 1889), particularly the opening movement of its final version, the one which started its life as part of the d minor quartet. This might at the same time help us to understand why Gade shifted this movement from one quartet to another.

It was obviously not because Gade considered it an artistically poor movement – had he done so, he would hardly have reused it.

Whereas the opening movement of the D major quartet is a clear-cut, straightforward sonata form, the opening movement of the e minor quartet displays a considerable number of atypical characteristics. As expected, the Exposition presents a first theme in e minor and a second theme, a song-like melody, in the relative key of G major, although the relative key does not emerge very clearly. The bridge-passage between the two themes is rather long with a considerably self-contained character. The Development section uses material from both the first theme and the bridge passage. Now follows – somewhat surprisingly – a presentation of the second theme in B major. The ensuing presentation of the main theme might be perceived as the beginning of the Recapitulation but is in fact the beginning of the Coda.

Three music examples will illustrate the romantic articulation of this movement. First the opening theme:

The following example shows a section of the bridge passage between the two themes:

And finally the second theme:

It is not at all farfetched to suggest that Gade transferred this movement from its original position as the opening of the later D major quartet to the more freely composed, more rhythmically ragged, more dramatic, more unconventional e minor quartet exactly because of its less formal, more romantic character. The first movement of the e minor quartet is a classical-romantic composition.

In addition, the genesis of the D major and the e minor quartets provides evidence for the fact that Gade was very conscious about the stylistic trappings of his works, and not, as suggested by some, a composer on automatic pilot with a fixed compositional procedure and an output of varying quality.

Other Retroclassicistic Works

There are a number of other instrumental compositions by Gade which may be labelled as retro-classicistic.

Symphony No. 4 in B flat major op. 20 (1850), a short symphony and a small orchestra (2 fl., 2 ob., 2 cl., 2 fg., 4 cor., 2 tr., timp. and strings). The musical expression is light and on the whole there are only a few romantic elements in this work. The symphony which was extremely popular in the second half of the 19th century has even been accused of not belonging to the serious symphonic genre, but rather of being a piece of popular music.

Piano trio in F major op. 42 (1864). Much of what has been said about the fourth symphony goes for the piano trio op. 42 as well. And it may be added that Gade's op. 42 differs greatly from Gade's other piano trio with regard to musical style, the *Novellettes* op. 29.

Novellettes for string orchestra in F major op. 53 (1874), while the *Novellettes for string orchestra* in E major op. 58 (1886) are better characterized as classical-romantic.

4.2 Cantata *Zion*, op. 49

Gade's op. 48[75], 49[76] and 50[77] form a cantata trilogy consisting of

op. 48: *Kalanus* (1867-68)
op. 49: *Zion* (1874)
op. 50: *The Crusaders* (1866)

Gade did not often write about the stylistics of his music. However, a letter to Raymond Härtel reads: "Zion, for choir, baritone solo and orchestra (text after motives from the Old Testament) op. 49. […] It belongs between 'Kalanus' and 'The Crusaders' as middle-section, although of a quite different character from the other two (their title-pages, however, must correspond)".[78]

"Of a quite different character" is not an unambiguous wording, and it is not inadmissible to interpret it as referring to musical style.

Kalanus and *The Crusaders* are definitely classical-romantic works, whereas *Zion* fits the characteristics of retro-classicism perfectly.

Zion has four movements:

1) Introduction
2) The Departure from Egypt
3) The Captivity in Babylon
4) The Return, Prophecy of the New Jerusalem

An example from each of the movements shall illustrate the musical style of *Zion*:

---

75. Niels W. Gade: WORKS, Series IV, Vol. 4, *Kalanus, Dramatisches Gedicht von Carl Andersen für Soli, Chor und Orchester*, op. 48.
76. Niels W. Gade: *Zion, Concertstück für Chor, Baryton-Solo und Orchester*, op. 49.
77. Niels W. Gade: *Die Kreuzfahrer, Dramatisches Gedicht von Carl Andersen für Soli, Chor und Orchester*, op. 50.
78. Inger Sørensen: *Niels W. Gade og hans europæiske kreds. En brevveksling 1836-1891*, Vol 2, No. 781 (letter from Gade to Raymond Härtel): Original German text: "Zion für Chor, Baryton Solo u Orchester (Text nach alttestamentlichen Motiven) Opus 49 […] Es gehört zwischen 'Kalanus' und 'Kreuzfahrer' als Mittelstück, doch in ganz anderen Character als die beiden genannten (Titelblatt soll für alle 3 übereinstimmen.)"

The opening bars of the Introduction:

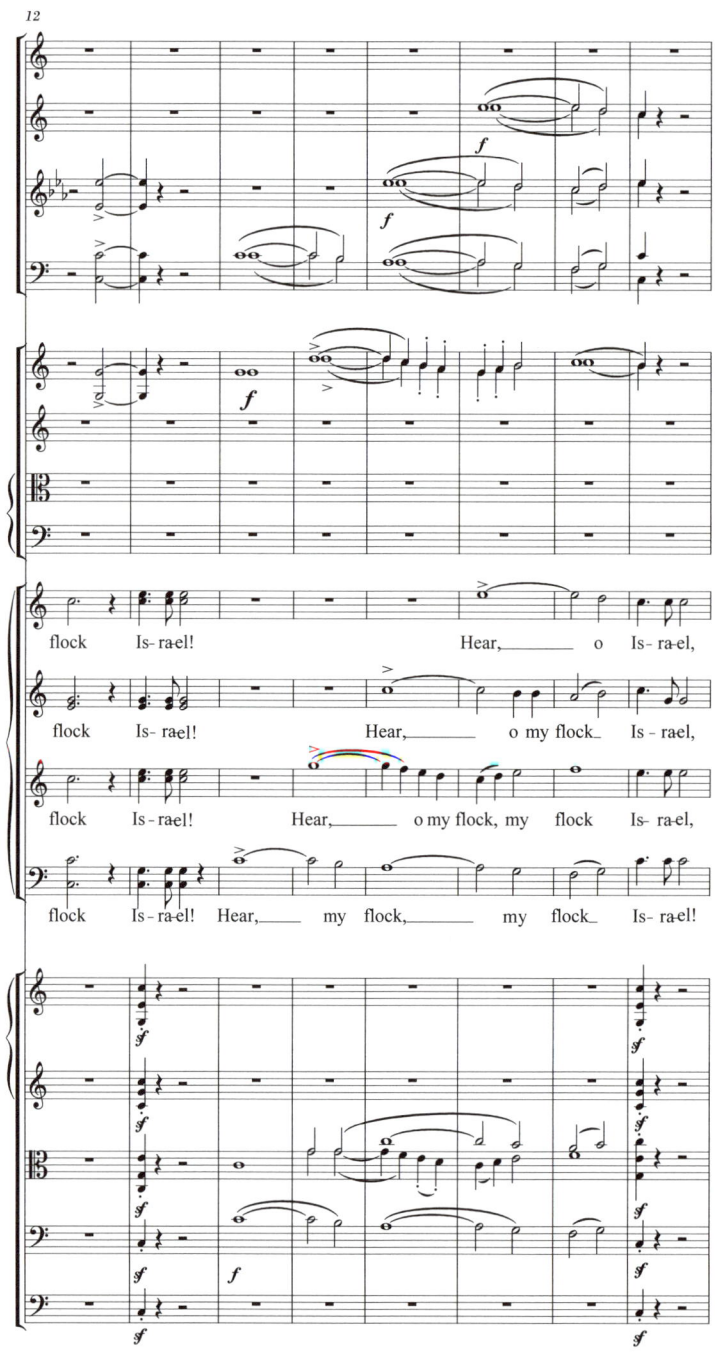

The Introduction and The Departure from Egypt are closely related musically. A more lyrical theme enters at bar 130 to the text: "Like as a flock He has gently led His people by Moses' and Aron's hand":

THE DEPARTURE FROM EGYPT

The Captivity in Babylon shows an interesting musical structure to the text: "So He made them to fall by the heathen" and "and their mighty foemen bow'd them down." Fundamentally the melodic lines in the chorus are the same for both parts of the text. But while that of the first is a straightforward and serene one that of the second is transformed by way of rhythm and especially orchestration to make it appear much more martial.

And from The Return the controlled, yet powerful annunciation of the coming of Christ with the striking effect of the trombones in bars 61 and 75 and the shift of metre.

5. Neo-classicism

The neo-classical composers such as Igor Stravinsky, Paul Hindemith and the French group Les Six are impossible to characterize precisely and exhaustively in a few words. Nevertheless, the following is a modest attempt to do so:

1) They compose within the boundaries of some tonal system.

In *Unterweisung im Tonsatz*[79] Paul Hindemith has presented a radical attempt to redefine the tonal system so that it covers not only cadential harmony but stretches its jurisdiction into the 20th century.

There is in an account like the present not room for a thorough scrutiny of the theoretical fundament of *Unterweisung*, which is both comprehensive and complex (and in several respects invites to contradiction). I must limit myself to a presentation of the most important of Hindemith's conclusions: He does not recognize a) that chords are built as stacks of thirds, b) the principle of inversion of chords and c) that of enharmonic equivalence. According to Hindemith a flat is always the same note as g sharp and any combination of notes represents a chord with one fundamental note. He gives a large table showing the hierarchy of chords. In the top-left corner of the following table, *Tabelle zur Akkordbestimmung*, you will find the chords of cadential harmony.

---

79. Paul Hindemith, *Unterweisung im Tonsatz, Theoretischer Teil*.

A Klänge ohne Tritonus

I Ohne Sekunden und Septimen

1. Grundton und Baßton sind derselbe

2. Grundton liegt höher im Akkord

III Mit Sekunden und Septimen

1. Grundton und Baßton sind derselbe

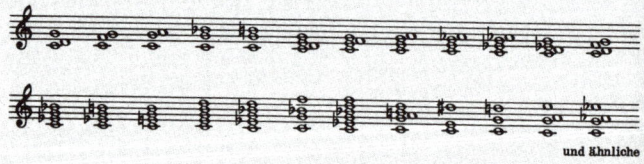

und ähnliche

2. Grundton liegt höher im Akkord

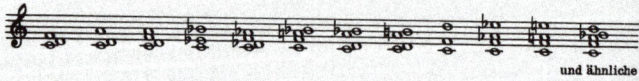

und ähnliche

V Unbestimmbar

B Klänge mit Tritonus

II Ohne kleine Sekunden und große Septimen.
Tritonus untergeordnet

   a Nur mit kleiner Septime (ohne große Sekunde)
      Grundton und Baßton sind derselbe

   b Mit großer Sekunde und kleiner Septime
     1. Grundton und Baßton sind derselbe

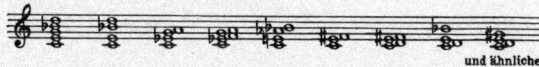

                                          und ähnliche

     2. Grundton liegt höher im Akkord

                                            und ähnliche

     3. Mit mehreren Tritoni

                       und ähnliche

IV Mit kleinen Sekunden und großen Septimen.
Ein Tritonus oder mehrere untergeordnet

   1. Grundton und Baßton sind derselbe

                                und ähnliche

   2. Grundton liegt höher im Akkord

                                  und ähnliche

VI Unbestimmbar. Tritonus übergeordnet

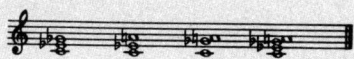

Stravinsky – in his *Poetics of Music* – rejects that his music should be labelled atonal: "the process is completed: the diatonic system has lived out its life cycle. The work of the Renaissance polyphonists had not yet entered into this system, and we have seen that the music of our time abides by it no longer. A parallel progression of ninth-chords would suffice as proof. It was here that the gates opened upon what has been labeled with the abusive term: *atonality*.

The expression is fashionable. But that doesn't mean that it is very clear. And I should like to know just what those persons who use the term mean by it. The negating prefix *a* indicates a state of indifference in regard to the term, negating without entirely renouncing it. Understood in this way, the word *atonality* hardly corresponds to what those who use it have in mind. If it were said that my music is atonal, that would be tantamount to saying that I had become deaf to tonality. Now it well may be that I remain for a considerable time within the bounds of the strict order of tonality, even though I may quite consciously break up this order for the purposes of establishing a new one. In that case I am not *a*tonal, but *anti*tonal. I am not trying to argue pointlessly over words: it is essential to know what we deny and what we affirm".[80]

Polytonality is a special application of tonal structures. It is applied by many neo-classicistic composers but is especially prominent with Darius Milhaud

---

80. Igor Stravinsky: *Poetics of Music* in the Form of Six Lessons, Preface by George Seferis, Translated by Arthus Knodel and Ingolf Dahl, Harvard University Press, Cambridge, Massachusetts;
Igor Stravinsky: *Poétique Musicale*, Harvard University Press, Cambridge, Massachusetts, Original French text: "le processus est accompli: le système tonal a vécu. L'œuvre des polyphonistes de la Renaissance n'entre pas encore dans ce système, et nous avons vu que la musique de notre temps n'y adhère plus. Une succession parallèle d'accords de *neuvième* suffirait à en donner la preuve.
C'est par là que la porte s'est ouverte sur ce qu'on a appelé d'un terme abusif: *atonalité*. L'expression est à la mode. Cela ne fait pas qu'elle soit bien claire. Et j'aimerais savoir comment l'entendent ceux qui l'emploient. L'*a* privatif indique un état d'indifférence à l'égard du terme qu'il annihile sans le désavouer. Ansi comprise, l'atonalité ne répond guère á ce qu'entendent ceux qui l'emploient. Si l'on disait de ma musique qu'elle est atonale, cela reviendrait à dire que je suis devenu sourd à la tonalité. Or il se peut que je me tienne plus ou moins longtemps dans l'ordre strict de la tonalité, quitte à le briser sciemment pour en établir un autre. Dans ce cas, je ne suis pas *atonal*, mais *antitonal*. Je ne fais pas ici une vaine querelle de mots: il est essentiel de savoir ce qu'on nie et ce qu'on affirme."

with whom we find this passage from the *Saudades do Brazil*, Suite de Danses No. 10, *Paineras*:[81]

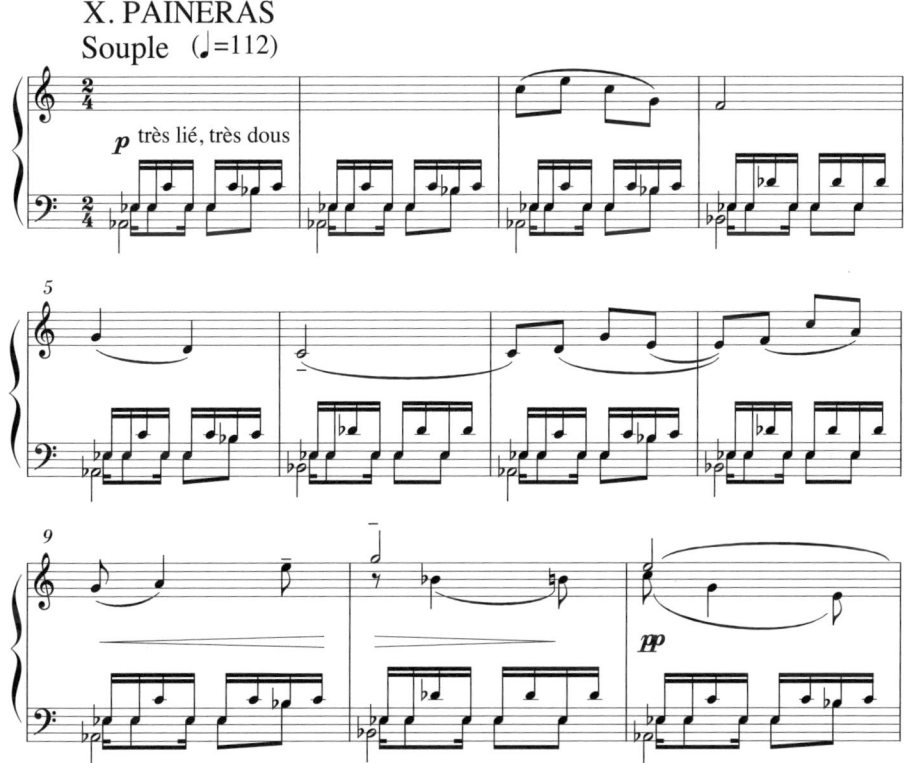

The right hand plays a melody in C major, while the left hand has an accompaniment displaying the tonal functions T and D in A flat major.

Here polytonality is applied with a purely aesthetical view without any extramusical connotations.

In the music examples below from Arthur Honnegers *Le Roi David*[82] No. 5 *Cortège* we find the following:

---

81. Darius Milhaud: *Saudades do Brazil*, Suite de Danses No. 10, *Paineras*.
82. Arthur Honegger: *Le Roi David*.

The bass is in f minor, discant in A major and D major played by two trumpets.

The bass is in f minor, discant in d minor played by a French horn. Bars 7-9 display the same musical material as bars 2-4.

The bass is in f minor, upper part played by a trombone in F sharp major.

The music displays a general crescendo, and at the culmination bars 19-21 we hear all four motives played in four different keys, evidently connotating the position of the individual army groups:

Certain types of tonality related to – but not identical with – Pre-baroque modality are also found in the neo-classicistic tonal toolbox.

Finally – especially in the 1920s – you encounter tonality bordering on atonality.

2) They profess to some sort of metrical rhythm, a rhythmical way of expression characterized by a significant distinction between strong and weak beats within a measure.

In principle a neo-classical composition may stay in 4/4 metre throughout. But a higher frequency of change of metre, and consequently more variation in the number of, and distance between, the strong beats is common. Especially with Stravinsky and Hindemith such changes of metre occur very frequently, less so with the French neo-classicists. A single music example from the first movement of Hindemith's *Sonata for Oboe and Piano* will serve as an example in point:[83]

---

83. Paul Hindemith: *Sonata for Oboe and Piano*.

Note the shift between 2/4 and 3/8 metre in the oboe, little rhythmic 'stumblings', while the piano at the same time remains in the steady-going 3/8 metre.

3) The neo-classical composers generally apply musical forms from the classical period, first and foremost the sonata form but also forms such as the chaconne and even older dance forms are applied by them. In this respect the neo-classicistic music is end-to-end with the classical-romantic music of the 19th century.

4) By way of musical expression the neo-classicists avoid strong emotions and aspire to coolness and objectivity but with musical humour as an important ingredient. The humoristic element in particular in much neo-classicistic music represents an important development compared with the music of the 19th century

On p. 73 we classified Saint-Saëns' *Septuor* op. 65 as a retro-classical work: but not only is the septet retro-classicistic in its way of musical expression, in addition it contains at least one truly neo-classical rhythmic trick in the Gavotte:

Were I to notate the beginning of the Gavotte by ear it would come out like this, interpreting the loud beats to be the strong beats of the metre:

No. 4, GAVOTTE ET FINAL (aural reproduction of score)

However, Saint-Saëns has notated it in this way:

No. 4, GAVOTTE ET FINAL

My version reveals the rhythmic trick that the quadruple metre is disturbed by a bar in 5/4 metre. But would Saint-Saëns have accepted my interpretation? In the Menuet (bars 42-45) of op. 65 a precursor of the rhythmic trick turns up

No. 2, MENUET
(Tempo di menuetto moderato)

with staccato on the first beat of the octave leap and an accent on the second. In my opinion this "warning" strengthens the analysis of the rhythmic trick in the Gavotte.

Although Stravinsky's *Histoire du Soldat* may not be considered a thorough-bred neo-classical composition, the style elements to be pointed out below may perfectly well serve as examples of neo-classical stylistics.

One of the most striking examples of this kind of rhythmic trick is found in the introduction to the *Marche Royale* of Stravinsky's *Histoire du Soldat*:[84]

---

84. Igor Stravinsky: *Histoire du Soldat*.

[Musical score: MARCHE ROYAL (♩=112)]

First, by notating the first bar as 5/8 Stravinsky evidently decided not to make things easier for the musicians. If he had notated the first bar with an upbeat in 2/4 some ambiguity would have been avoided – at least in the trombone:

(MARCHE ROYAL)

The musicians would then immediately perceive note 2 as the strong beat in 2/4, which would prevent ambiguity until the second 5/8 (bar 9).

The situation is somewhat different from the listener's point of view. He will probably direct his attention to the equidistant fortissimo (or forte) quaver chords, which are consistently separated by quaver rests. The listener is – at least to begin with – bound to perceive the chords as falling on the strong beats. But after a couple of bars he will be in doubt, because this interpretation forces him to interpret the crotchets in the trombone as syncopations. But any conventional understanding of the melody will interpret the crotchets as falling on the beats, not between them. In this rhythmic conflict between chords and melody, the melody will emerge victorious for most listeners – probably because the chords can, without much resistance, come to be interpreted as upbeats. It was, after all, only their bombastic accentuation at the very beginning of the march that caused the chords to be interpreted as the strong beats. But with the next 5/8 bar the relative rhythmic stability is again disturbed. The final note itself (note 1 in bar 10) in the melody as well as in the chords must be interpreted as falling on a strong beat, which means that the rhythmic status of the chords must once again be changed.

The opening of the *Marche Royale* is a true study in conflicting rhythmic signals.

As regards tonality the trombone melody sticks by and large to B flat major in the first 6-7 bars, the only disturbing element being the a flat in bar 1. In bars 8-9 it is as if Stravinsky intends to end the melody in C major, i.e. on the last note in bar 9. But the actual final note (bar 10, note 1) very abruptly forces the melody back to B flat major.

The chord structures are unconventional too. The pedal point on d, in violin and double bass, does not send a clear signal as to the tonal orientation of the music, and the d also disturbs the otherwise clear succession of chords, which oscillates between a tonic and a dominant in B flat major.

In my personal opinion the opening of the Gavotte in Saint-Saëns' op. 65 is a deliberate rhythmic trick of Saint-Saëns, even if it is far less sophisticated than that of Stravinsky in his *Marche Royale*.

Saint-Saëns' *Le Carnaval des Animaux*[85] was written in 1886 but apart from a few performances around that time Saint-Saëns laid down a performance veto and also prohibited the work from being published before his death.

What makes this *Grande Fantasie Zoologique* a composition to be taken seriously is paradoxically the humour that saturates the work from first to last in several different guises.

The following is by no means a complete list, merely a few relevant examples:

---

85. See page 74.

1) The slowest of animals, *Tortues*, is depicted by a slow tempo presentation of Offenbach's *Can-can* (No. 4).
2) The animals of the carnival include *Pianistes* (No. 11) and *Personnages à longues oreilles* (No. 8)
3) The *Pianistes* play, not a piece of actual piano music, but a scale exercise successively raised by a semitone, *ad modum* Czerny.
4) Risking a conviction of treachery against French cultural heritage, I finally claim that the voluptuous melodic line of *Le Cygne* is a humorous comment on romantic exaggeration.

On the purely musical level *Le Carnaval des Animaux* displays some neo-classicist traits, particularly in the realm of harmony, with many instances of freely handled dissonances, not encountered in 19th-century retro-classicism. In this connection our music example from the first movement of his 2nd string quartet should also be mentioned.

6. Parenthesis on the Danish composer Paul von Klenau (1883-1946)

After having studied composition with Danish Otto Malling around 1900, Klenau moved to Berlin to continue his studies under Max Bruch. For a period shortly after World War I he studied with Schönberg, and there are elements of 12-tone technique in his works.

Some of his instrumental works have recently been published by the Danish Centre for Music Editing (DCM).

His ambitious *Symphony No. 9*, for choir, soli and orchestra to a Latin text containing quotations from the Catholic *Requiem Mass* came out in 2014.

His *Symphony No. 8*,[86] which is inscribed "Im alten Stil" (In Olden Style) on the first page of the manuscript score, was published in 2017. Written in 1942, it would supposedly have been written in some neo-classicistic dialect.

However, an analysis reveals very little, if anything, that goes beyond the retro-classicistic works of the 19th century presented in this article. Furthermore, Klenau's *Symphony No. 8* is a rather poor composition, and why Klenau wrote it at all remains – at least for the time being – an unanswered question.

---

86. Paul von Klenau: *Symphony No. 8*.

7. Conclusion

The above survey has – in my opinion – established the existence of musical works (or single movements) with such a retrospective stylistic appearance that it justifies the application of the term retro-classicism (retro-baroque, retro-renaissance). Nor do I doubt that the composers in question have been conscious about the retrospective character of these works. In other words: We are not dealing with statistical variations in the musical style of these composers.

The analyses of the works of two of the greatest French composers of the second half of the 19th century in particular bear witness to the fact that the antiromantic strain in their respective *œuvre* is consciously produced and represents works, which in no way may be claimed to be of a lesser artistic value than their classical-romantic works.

As to the reason, or motive, for this choice of style, I think that with the classical-romantic composers there was always a touch of anti-romanticism, a proclivity to react against romantic gigantism, and this anti-romantic inclination sows the seeds of 20th-century neo-classicism.

Furthermore, I am convinced, that retro-classicistic works, movements and passages can be found in the *œuvre* of many other classical-romantic composers than the three treated here.

We are not talking about a joint, let alone organized, movement, and this fact corroborates the conception of a latent but omnipresent reaction against the romantic cornucopia.

It was Mr. wrong-note-Prokofiev's *Symphonie Classique*, which in history writing came to represent the swing of the pendulum towards neo-classicism. Rightly considered, however, the retrospective stylistics with Saint-Saëns, Gounod, Niels Gade and probably many others is an equally, if not more, important heralding of 20th-century neo-classicism.

List of quoted literature

Apel, Willy: *The Harvard Dictionary of Music*, Heinemann, London 1944.

Fallon, Daniel Martin: *The Symphonies and Symphonic Poems of Camille Saint-Saëns*, A Dissertation Presented to the Faculty of the Graduate School of Yale University in Candidacy for the Degree of Doctor of Philosophy, December 1973.

Gads Musikleksikon, edited by Finn Gravesen and Martin Knakkergaard, G.E.C. Gad, Copenhagen 2003.

Grout, Donald Jay and Palisca, Claude V.: *A History of Western Music*, fifth Edition, W.W. Norton & Company, New York 1996.

Hindemith, Paul: *Unterweisung im Tonsatz, Theoretischer Teil*, Mainz 1940.

Hyperion CDA6743 1/2: Camille Saint-Saëns: *Piano Quartet, Piano Quintet, Septuor, Sonata for Oboe & Piano, Sonata for Clarinet & Piano, Sonata for Bassoon & Piano, Caprice, Tarantelle* with the Nash Ensemble. Liner notes by Sabina Teller Ratner, 2005.

Die Musik in Geschichte und Gegenwart, Bärenreiter-Verlag, Kassel 1949-1986.

Musikproduktion Dabringhaus und Grimm MDG 604 0590-2: Camille Saint-Saëns: *Etudes op. 52, 111, Album pour Piano op. 72* with Mi-Joo Lee, Piano. Liner notes by Ulrich Mahlert (translated by Susan Marie Praeder), 1995.

The New Grove Dictionary of Music and Musicians, edited by Stanley Sadie, Macmillan Publishers Limited, London 1980.

Saint-Saëns, Camille: *Musical Memories*, Translated by Edwin Gile Rich, Da Capo Press, New York 1969.

Saint-Saëns, Camille: *Outspoken Essays on Music*, Authorised Translation by Fred Rothwell, Greenwood Press, Publishers, Westport, Connecticut, reprint 1970.

Sohlmans Musiklexikon, Sohlmans Förlag AB, Stockholm 1975-79.

Stravinsky, Igor: *Poetics of Music* in the Form of Six Lessons, Preface by George Seferis, Translated by Arthus Knodel and Ingolf Dahl, Harvard University Press, Cambridge, Massachusetts 1947.

Stravinsky, Igor: *Poétique Musicale*, Harvard University Press, Cambridge, Massachusetts 1942.

Sørensen, Inger: *Niels W. Gade og hans europæiske kreds. En brevveksling 1836-1891*, Museum Tusculanum, Copenhagen 2008.

Sørensen, Søren; Christiansen, John; Marschner, Bo; Slumstrup, Finn: *Musikalske Begreber*, G.E.C. Gad, Copenhagen 1983.

List of music editions

Time of creation and publication of the works listed below largely derive from:

Sabina Teller Ratner: *Camille Saint-Saëns 1835-1921, A Thematic Catalogue of his Complete Works,* Volume 1, The Instrumental Works, Oxford University Press 2002.

The Grove Music Online.

The New Grove Dictionary of Music and Musicians edited by Stanley Sadie, Macmillan Publishers Limited, London 1980.

Dan Fog: *Niels W. Gade Katalog,* Verzeichnis der im Druck Erschienenen Kompositionen von Niels W. Gade (1817-1890), Dan Fog Musikforlag, København 1986.

KVK – Karlsruhe Virtual Catalog (internet database).

Gade, Niels W.: WORKS, Series II, Vol. 2, *The String Quartets,* Copenhagen 1996, Distribution Engstrøm & Sødring A/S Musikforlag, Bärenreiter Verlag.

Gade, Niels W.: WORKS, Series IV, Vol. 4, *Kalanus, Dramatisches Gedicht von Carl Andersen für Soli, Chor und Orchester op. 48,* Copenhagen 2018, Distribution Engstrøm & Sødring A/S Musikforlag, Bärenreiter Verlag.

Gade, Niels W.: *Zion, Concertstück für Chor, Baryton-Solo und Orchester op. 49,* Leipzig 1877.

Gade, Niels W.: *Die Kreuzfahrer, Dramatisches Gedicht von Carl Andersen für Soli, Chor und Orchester op. 50,* Breitkopf & Härtel, Leipzig 1866.

Gounod, Charles: *Petite Symphonie pour une Flûte, deux Hautbois, deux Clarinettes, deux Cors et deux Bassons,* Éditions Billaudot, Paris 1904.

Gounod, Charles: *1re Symphony in D,* Colombier, Paris 1855 (not available). Edition by Kalmus without pl. no.

Gounod, Charles: *Deuxième Symphonie en Mi bémol,* Éditions Choudens, Paris 2010?

Gounod, Charles: *Cäcilienmesse, Messe solenelle de Sainte Cécile,* Partitur neu eingerichtet und herausgegeben von Elmar Schloter, Musiverlag Max Hieber (MH 7006), München © 1983.

Gounod, Charles: *Quatrième Messe Solennelle, Messe Chorale sur l'intonation de la Liturgie Catholique,* Au Ménestrel, Heugel, Paris 1870.

Gounod, Charles: *Messe No. 5 in C, aux séminaires,* edited by Manfred Frank, Carus-Verlag 40.831/01, Stuttgart 1992.

Gounod, Charles: *Requiem in C, op. posth.,* Carus-Verlag, Carus 27.315, Stuttgart 2011.

Gounod, Charles: *The Seven Words of Our Saviour Upon the Cross*, Edited by Joseph Barnby, Novello and Co., London 1865.

Gounod, Charles: *Mors et Vita, A Sacred Trilogy*, Vocal Score with Pianoforte Accompaniment, Arranged from the Orchestral Score by O.B. Brown, Novello and Co., London 1885.

Gounod, Charles: *Gallia, Lamentation*, Partition Chant et Piano, Paris, Choudens, Paris 1871.

Gounod, Charles: *La Rédemption, Trilogie Sacrée*, Partition pour Chant et Piano Reduite par Berthold Tours, Novello and Co., London 1882?.

Hindemith, Paul: *Sonata for Oboe and Piano*, Edition Schott 3676, Mainz © 1939.

Honegger, Arthur: *Le Roi David*, Verlag Gebrüder Fœtisch, Lausanne 1952, reprint.

Klenau, Paul von: *Symphony No. 8*, Edited by Niels Krabbe, Danish Centre for Music Editing (DCM), Copenhagen 2017.

Milhaud, Darius: *Saudades do Brazil, Suite de Danses No. X Paineras*, Editions Max Eschig, Paris 2006.

Saint-Saëns, Camille: *Ire Symphonie op. 2*, S. Richault, Paris 1855.

Saint-Saëns, Camille: *Symphonie en Fa, "Urbs Roma" (1856)*, Édition Françaises de Musiques, Paris 1915. Printed from the same plates: Gerard Billaudot Éditeur Successeur, Paris 1974.

Saint-Saëns, Camille: *2e Symphonie op. 55*, Durand, Paris 1878.

Saint-Saëns, Camille: *3e Symphonie op. 78*, Durand, Paris 1886.

Saint-Saëns, Camille: *Suite pour Orchestre op. 49*, Durand, Paris 1877.

Saint-Saëns, Camille: *Premier Concerto pour Piano avec Accompagnement d'Orchestre op. 17*, Durand, Paris 1875.

Saint-Saëns, Camille: *2e Concerto pour Piano avec Accompagnement d'Orchestre op. 22*, Durand, Paris 1875.

Saint-Saëns, Camille: *3e Concerto pour Piano avec Accompagnement d'Orchestre op. 29*, Durand, Paris 1876.

Saint-Saëns, Camille: *4e Concerto pour Piano avec Accompagnement d'Orchestre op. 44*, Durand, Paris 1877.

Saint-Saëns, Camille: *5e Concerto Piano avec Accompagnement d'Orchestre op. 103*, Durand, Paris 1896.

Saint-Saëns, Camille: *Six Études pour Piano op. 52*, Durand, Paris 1877.

Saint-Saëns, Camille: *Six Études pour Piano op. 111*, Durand, Paris 1899.

Saint-Saëns, Camille: *Six Études pour la main gauche seule op. 135*, Durand, Paris 1912-13.

Saint-Saëns, Camille: *[Ire] Quatuor pour 2 Violons, Alto et Violoncelle op. 112*, Durand, Paris 1899.

Saint-Saëns, Camille: *2e Quatuor pour 2 Violons, Alto et Violoncelle op. 153*, Durand, Paris 1919.

Saint-Saëns, Camille:: *[Ire] Trio pour piano, violin et violoncelle op. 18*, J. Maho, Paris 1867.

Saint-Saëns, Camille: *Septuor pour Trompette, deux Violons, Alto, Violoncelle, Contrebasse et Piano op. 65*, Durand, Paris 1881.

Saint-Saëns, Camille: *Le Carnaval des Animaux*, Durand, Paris 1922.

Saint-Saëns, Camille: *2e Sonate pour Violoncelle et Piano op. 123*, Durand, Paris 1905.

Saint-Saëns, Camille: *Sonate pour Hautbois avec Accompagnement de Piano op. 166*, Durand, Paris 1921.

Saint-Saëns, Camille: *Sonate pour Clarinette avec Accompagnement de Piano op. 167*, Durand, Paris 1921.

Saint-Saëns, Camille: *Sonate pour Basson avec Accompagnement de Piano op. 168*, Durand, Paris 1921.

Stravinsky, Igor: *Histoire du Soldat*, Chester, London © 1924.